Invisible City

volumes in the collection of current poetry
edited by John McBride & Paul Vangelisti

Paralielata

noèun'altra

sampellegri

altosa, gluzè

ipastanaril

domenica,'i

heser eint

cchioacqua

Italian Poetry, 1960–1980: from Neo to Post Avant-garde

edited by Adriano Spatola & Paul Vangelisti

Invisible City | 2
San Francisco & Los Angeles

A grant from the Italian Ministry of Foreign Affairs
(thru the Italian Cultural Institute: San Francisco office,
Francesca Valente, director) aided the translation of
this anthology.

Grants from the Coordinating Council of Literary Magazines
and the National Endowment for the Arts (a federal agency)
aided the publication of this volume.

Front cover & frontispiece: Zeroglyph by Adriano Spatola
Back cover (paper edition only) photo by William Xerra
Press-mark by Giovanni Anceschi
Designed by John McBride
& printed in the United States

Library of Congress card catalog number 82-80897

ISBN 0-88031-060-X (paper)
ISBN 0-88031-061-8 (cloth)

Invisible City / Red Hill Press
PO Box 2853
San Francisco, California 94126

Introduction

The points of reference for this anthology are several recent publications that determine the limits and significance of our selection. First is the anthology *Poesia degli anni settanta* (Feltrinelli, 1979), edited by Antonio Porta; and the collection *Il movimento della poesia italiana negli anni settanta* (Dedalo, 1979), edited by Tomaso Kemeny and Cesare Viviani, which resulted from a conference on contemporary poetry held in Milano. There are at least two other anthologies, *Poesia italiana oggi* (Newton Compton, 1981), edited by Mario Lunetta, and *Chi è il poeta* (Gammalibri, 1980), edited by Silvia Batisti and Mariella Bettarini, that proved noteworthy.

In all these cases, the material presented sheds a notable light on the facts and intentions of Italian poetry in the last 20 years. These collections seem to possess simultaneously an inclusive and descriptive spirit while tending toward rhetorical excess and some argumentation verging on absurdity. However, the reader who seeks in these volumes a new tension in the poetry of the 70s may certainly be perplexed. Today this tension is the true and secret hope of all critics like ourselves who prefer research to immobility. Perhaps this tension remains unrealized because Italian poetry of the last decade expended enormous energy in two opposite bursts: the attempt to face and condense social reality, and the desire to flee this reality and create for the poet a 'private niche.'

Because of these considerations, we think this anthology ought to exclude any prophetic tone; our project closes rather than opens a period. We find this common not only to anthologies published in Italy but also to certain recent collections of Italian poetry published in the US.[1] Feldman's and Swann's is an anthology that respects, with much scrupulosity and perhaps a few inexactitudes, the panorama of Italian poetry as it might appear to serious scholars, however academic. The two collections of Ballerini and Milazzo are, instead, more steeped in linguistic experimentation. Obviously this is also our position, but with a significant difference. Like Ballerini and Milazzo we are committed to both criticism and poetry (a situation not rare in contemporary letters). But it seems that our colleagues, Ballerini and Milazzo, have dreamt, almost *wished,* an idea of poetry, especially in the case of 'The Waters of Casablanca.' We, instead, have tried more pragmatically to describe without dreaming, and to love with more reserve.

An example of this reserve is the way in which we approached the problem of translation. Adriano's notion was that each poet ought to select his own texts *in translation,* while Paul wanted to maintain some unity of style in view of the problems an American reader might have with the texts. Obviously we chose both solutions.

In fact, there are in this collection certain texts that are difficult reading while others prove difficult to interpret, even though they might appear at first more accessible. In Italian poetry of the last 20 years, direct language is not always spoken language, and indirect language is not always that of the written word.

This is also evident in the language of visual poetry. We included visual poetry in our selection not only as documentation of an important international poetic phenomenon but also because it seems to us that visual poetry continues to destroy the archetypes of Italian poetry.

As a more tangential point of reference, we kept in mind an anthology edited by Adriano for the Yugoslavian magazine *La Battana* (nos 16–17, 1968; no 20, 1969). Among the 'new poets' presented then almost in preview were writers who today occupy a substantial place in contemporary Italian poetry. Then, perhaps, the vocation of prophet was an easier one. But even in the present selection we have placed our bets, attempting to verify the *active variants* of a complex phenomenon that occurred after 1968, a date many critics consider a crossroads in Italian poetry. *Active variants* in that poetry today appear cut loose from the context that produces it, suspended in an air both rarefied and ahistorical. *Active variants* in that it seems necessary to many contemporary poets to regain a method of poetic research that is in a true sense *global.*[3] *Active variants* insofar as the creative mechanism appears too often jammed with the 'triumphant ego.'

The poetry of the 70s appears to have sought to cancel its debts to the poetry of the 60s. Here the observation seems to us rather obvious, though the term 'debts' is not exact enough. We are dealing with a more ambiguous rapport between these two periods. The Italian neo-avantgarde, which took off from the anthology *I Novissimi* in 1961,[4] attempted to involve poetry in its own linguistic maneuvers and the re-invention of the historical avantgarde; however, it reserved for its own domain a certain circumscribed space and specific passions. The neo-avantgarde re-invigorated certain *-isms* while reveling in irony and freedom from the schools of art. Undoubtedly in organizing Gruppo 63 it sought a privileged laboratory,[5] though at the same time this laboratory remained open and accessible. Thus the 'debts' to be cancelled were above all those of experience, both technical and organizational, not 'debts' exclusively circumscribed by the written word.

Our anthology signals a logical revision of this cultural utopia. In this we have tried to follow a process from its origins, through its development and eventual self-destruction, and even to the refusal of this neo-avantgarde utopia by a 'new' generation. The 'new' generation, in the anthology *La parola innamorata* (Feltrinelli, 1978), pretended to organize itself into a group, either for reasons of fun or defiance, or perhaps only as a camouflage. It is no wonder that the two editors, Giancarlo Pontiggia and Enzo Di Mauro, worked from the inside out, gathering around themselves a mass of illusions and self-compliments, impulsiveness and silence.

Obviously it seems that now the concept of a group can only exist based on a confidence in the rites of the historical avantgarde. Confidence or faith? The answer is always ambiguous or may often depend – as is the case of the anthology *Il pubblico della poesia*[6] – less on the question of literary tendencies than on that of sociological preoccupations. Here, in fact, it is the specter of the public that forms the hypothetical group which the poet turns to. From this specter comes the notion of a neo-decadent isolation of the poet and the uniqueness of his life.

In 1976 in two issues of *Il Verri* (vol 5, nos 1 & 2), Luciano Anceschi proposed a reconsideration of poetry's 'precarious equilibriums.' Precarious in the diversity of various critical and poetic positions, but even the actual obsessiveness of certain *apodictical* formulations. Precarious, in a positive way, because born of this situation, above all, with the aid of the habitual phenomenology of Anceschi, and not determined or decided *a priori*. Finally, an incurable precariousness of a poetry corroded by its own poisons and disguises, and occasionally stripped bare of the loquaciousness of its own self-interrogation.

We find toward the middle of the 70s a period of definite transition, a not very happy one for Italian poetry. However, certain magazines – we cite *Tam Tam* and *Pianura* – had already tried to establish a method of poetry constructed from the contexts of poetry itself, in an autonomous use of dates and ideas. The relationship becomes one not between poet and public, certainly not a carnal one. Instead, the only possible relationship becomes that of the poet with his devices, and ultimately with a text that talks of itself.

– *Adriano Spatola*
Paul Vangelisti

---

1. *Italian Poetry Today,* ed. Ruth Feldman & Brian Swann (New Rivers, 1979); 'Italian Post-Modernist Writing,' Luigi Ballerini & Richard Milazzo, *Shantih* (Summer–Fall 1978); 'The Waters of Casablanca,' Ballerini & Milazzo, *Chelsea 37* (1978).
2. There was a third notion, Giulia Niccolai's, who started the project with us but for reasons of her own work had to drop out. Given Giulia's remarkable bilingualism the problem for her was not one of direct translation but of 'thinking of' Italian poetry in American terms. It appears to us that Giulia resolved this problem in her excellent translation of Gertrude Stein's *A Geographical History of America* (La Tartaruga, 1980).

3. Cf. Adriano's *Verso la poesia totale* ('Toward a Total Poetry'), Paravia (1978); Vicenzo Accame's *Il segno poetico* ('The Poetic Sign'), Samedane, Munt Press (1977); Luigi Ballerini's *La piramide capovolta* ('The Upsidedown Pyramid'), Marsilio (1975); and Lamberto Pignotti's *La scrittura verbo-visiva* (*'Verbal-Visual Writing'*), Espresso Strumenti (1980).

4. *I Novissimi,* ed. by Alfredo Giuliani, containing poems and texts by Nanni Balestrini, Alfredo Giuliani, Elio Pagliarani, Antonio Porta and Edoardo Sanguineti (first edition, Rusconi e Paolazzi, 1961, Einaudi, 1965).

5. *Gruppo 63,* ed. by Giuliani and Balestrini, Feltrinelli (1964); *Gruppo 63: Critica e teoria,* ed. by Renato Barilli and Angelo Guglielmi, Feltrinelli (1976).

6. ('Poetry's Public'), ed. Franco Cordelli & Alfonso Berardinelli, Lerici (1975).

Italian Poetry, 1960–1980:
from Neo to Post Avant-garde

Vincenzio Accame / Marcello Angioni / Nanni Balestrini
Luigi Ballerini / Dino Bedino / Gianfranco Baruchello
Franco Beltrametti / Mirella Bentivoglio / Gianni Bertini
Irma Blank / Tomaso Binga / Edoardo Cacciatore
Nanni Cagnone / Luciano Caruso / Giorgio Celli
Agostino Contò / Corrado Costa / Maurizio Cucchi
Michelangelo Coviello / Betty Danon / Milo De Angelis
Enzo Di Mauro / Giuliano Della Casa / Fabio Doplicher
Flavio Ermini / Gilberto Finzi / Giovanni Fontana
Luigi Fontanella / Biancamaria Frabotta / Alfredo Giuliani
Milli Graffi /Giuliano Gramigna / Massimo Gualtieri
Giuseppe Guglielmi / Tomaso Kemeny / Giulio Leoni
Arrigo Lora-Totino / Nino Majellaro / Lucia Marcucci
Angelo Maugeri / Stelio Martini / Eugenio Miccini
Giuseppe Morrocchi / Maurizio Nannucci / Giulia Niccolai
Martino Oberto / Piera Oppezzo / Luciano Ori
Elio Pagliarini / Anna Oberto / Renzo Paris
Claudio Parmiggiani / Lamberto Pignotti / Raffaele Perrotta
Giancarlo Pontiggia / Antonio Porta / Mario Ramous
Vittorio Reta / Franco Rella / Giovanni Sandri
Amelia Rosselli / Edoardo Sanguineti / Aldo Selleri
Gregorio Scalise / Carlo Sitta / Adriano Spatola
Paolo Valesio / Franco Verdi / Sebastiano Vassalli
Patrizia Vicinelli / Carlo Villa / Emilio Villa
Luigi Viola / Cesare Vivaldi / Cesare Viviani
William Xerra

Vincenzo Accame

[*Tre capitoli per un trattato*]

Marcello Angioni

Wasithim / Twashim
(or Notes on mind's dialogic nature)

Interobduction:
>   The procedure's formalization is compulsory and
recognized as such. One cannot obviously recede to antecedent fashions
in order to think here and now.
The only consolation in the horrible righteousness of the present
situation is the awareness that poetry always celebrates the prostitrusion
of barkness.

Wasithim, gamucking the scales, gothingly diverting the bing from the
bale, diverting much fooking from lurking or resoaking, opens the
prodroem:

> *I'm set a subject*
> *mejet De Sonset*
> *mustang't by defination*
> *restrain the stake in*
> *upjects that ichnore*
> *an ardently persistent strenuous*
> *procopstination penshive*
> *point pour poise jesture*
> *can her burgh asloppy*
> *abersleepy norm act* TV *t*
> *poasture fromm onun*
> *can scale nor remercible ramp*

Twashim, refusing both gabook and retrousy, feelactic and fairly
mingus, rawtorious by chance, nor ever seeking deedawnical situations
or notouations, thus propounds:

> *or ditto prawnpoised come own*
> *fellowtonic cinderpusslentimental*
> *come say abreath soothlee*
> *a day joe forever always lo*
> *on some billimetric discunt*
> *ceasing ho don't dare roastercrack*
> *can four seas leduc sum pea mien tows*
> *don't dare roastercrack on the selves*
> *bertenders barsearchers cuntenders*
> *snoboddi privy ends me from fleeking*
> *not eaves those bestyards of yore*

Desertically voiced:

Poetry doesn't appear to be the best way to overcome
fear for death. We must eliminate all possible forms
of inner topics from our universe of discourse.
The prevailing ideologies are more than sufficient
for this purpose. Our task is precise and merciless :
we are bound to occupy, without any further delay,
the intersection point between zero and one.

Twashim, backlusciously backfeedingly sour:

not finding the plaice they sooked
grinding forth the fairce they dilooted
they stooded and they brooded
winniever they poohded
far never readounding so crooded . . .

After some hesitation, steadfastly Manon Tropical:

don't believe uhm real pussiballic
clamation withal he's De Con
abstractilodactilo phoneycal
removal Du Pre, sir, sinfaunical
not even purr plexus psaltonical
we canned but don't wonned simply crownical

Desertically voiced number two:

How shall we attack ? How shall we force It to
reveal us some coordinates ?
Strategies and tactics belong to the operational
sector, they require a visualization of the problem,
a vectorial somatization, as it were.
I gotta feeling . . .

Redundant Wasithim:

I put a jaure intend and see :
raw end eat wash pop on eye ill
not to cuntinue on this frill
I have to peirce on every step
asander torn from moaney a shelling
and barray more plus sickamore
cunoutrange the feelanchore
here comes my nore and hiss my jaure
and see twat ill (oh, moan) she ignore

Twashim, openly showing deterioration of some levels of dialogic
fairness, doesn't refrain from personal attacks, with the following
result:

true coo lent us
is nut a tree but not right proper
molly sanderskine soap ragmentes

caldimethal extra for biddities
we not acceipt those sheiks con oddi
ties have jusself it and vial
repeet thighsss . . .

Ages later, remunchingly crunching:

not can indent thus
cannot ten tit tend us
La Croona is *La Creena*
the support's trancelesson
fawllen chimaerae in prescription
sacrilegified for the abullition
the cymbd's and the qyadratic's
rioteries without conneries
lasshivious exponents of silly johnmetrics

Twashim seeks the end of dispute and argument, tries an exit dignified, momentous and more than that, but fatigue's alurking and . . .

with these words, postambulary
goes the coarse from all'n to gary
chained to blablasphumus very
licensing and licensong
we perdour toot all along
if they ask what is wrong
we'll stay cute like a womb
now alas the mouse is gorely
redescends to the fourlorely
we regard it go newborely
and we finish our popcorely

Finale, tutti:

feeling fairly gary
getting core, man, snide her
all'n' seed, you know
travails fustian moanments
gets afaust, königsbergs high king
all'n' seed, you should know
letaliously disgracing all sorts
rebooks his sorely corely lorely gary
a dry and spate (oh, la la), man,
burrows many a day, my laidi
julipear a nickel (ahi, ahi, ahi,)
costs twhat costs, corrugations of ribs
torenado always trams at belly
frankly etching jorny johnbone
de parme

Nanni Balestrini

Living in Milan

If somewhere around there's a psychia trist for Milan please will he step f orward the problem is this there are two cities one works or is out of wor read them when.... this is a ghost s tory they are aggressive and violent ghosts who smash plate glass window s with stones and use iron bars again st the smartest cars what hides them taking advantage of the fact that an employee was going in through a doorw ay that had been closed up until then the group rushed in shouting in the r k puts up with the drain of inflation can't find a home and sees pictures i n the papers of millionaires arrested and then let out on bail for next to from people's eyes are not curtains b ut police tear-gas eight or ten at mo st left the march and attack a shop an d burst into an office plate glass wi oom some employees were working the e arlier one was flung against the wall while the aggressor cut the telephone wires smashed two plate glass windows nothing yet continues to muster up st rength cut down and at most put toget her a series of political gripes whic h are then settled peacefully and the ndows smash into pieces counters and desks are turned over papers set on f ire simple slogans written on the wal ls it all lasts only a few minutes ca with crowbars and then threw four mol otov cocktails two exploded starting a small fire which was then put out b y the fire brigade yelling blacklegs re's a second Milan far smaller even if far noisier which seems like it's going mad on certain occasions and do esn't cut down but blows up with mo uses a great fright considerable dama ge injured hardly ever do the ghosts go unarmed often not even masked and they don't threaten anyone they hit a blacklegs the commando ran away and t hen dispersed in the narrow streets o f the area other employees and bosses from the five floors above hurried mo

lotov cocktails and expects to settle accounts right away but almost always calculates wrongly and sometimes pick s on the wrong adversary when it does n't run off like an old ghost but wit h one difference their sheets are red they are the dramatic personae of the Sunday of violence the day came to a wn since they feared a far greater fi re the explosion of the fire bombs des troyed two terminals of the computer counters papers desks at 10.25 twenty n't end up with fighting alongside th e adversary if there is a psychiatris t for Milan the problem for him is as follows that these two Milans are so dignified end with the youths grouped around the Palalido who were charged by the police after a vain attempt to break through the gates to listen to or so people burst into the sales off ice of Dalmine on the sixth floor in Via Larga 23 the fifteen employees we re forced to leave at 10,30 a great n metimes one and the same Milan one li ves within the other there's no divid ing line or if there is it passes wit hin one and the same social set midst a concert without paying they got the ir anger out of their systems by damag ing four cars of the flying squad and injuring half a dozen policemen and n umber of youth broke into the buildi ng of the Riunione Adriatica Insuranc e Company in Corso Italia 23 the empl oyees had to stop working however in people who know each other sometimes in the same families it's like a body with two heads one no longer has any idea what the other is up to greater arabinieri to try to give a face to t he ghost so as to see what there is u nder their red sheets how can you rep ly this furious attack intensifying f the meantime the doorman closed the e xits automatically and somebody calle d the police thirteen extremists are cornered and taken to the police head Milan which reasons looks with astoni

shment and then irritation and then d
ismay upon the microscopic Milan whi
ch now and then goes wild and the Mil
or workers in large factories the str
uggle against restructurization and f
or a guaranteed wage taking up intern
al demonstrations again and the punis
quarters they are let out on bail cha
rged with breaking and entering half
an hour later hundreds of demonstrator
s from extremist groups meet up outsi
an which goes wild seems to be moved
by forces which are more and more dif
ficult to classify because they are a
lmost always tied up with the particu
hment of the big chiefs bringing the
matter into the streets where instead
it's a question of workers from small
factories their answers to sacking fi
de the RAS and hold up the traffic up
until the afternoon demanding the rel
ease of those held in custody at 10.4
5 the most serious episode of the day
lar problem or linked by odd connecti
ons to more than one problem which in
themselves ought not to lead to these
cases of group hysteria and these exp
nally consolidating in the various di
stricts the reappropriation of reduce
d wages of rates and rents with taking
thirty or so people with handkerchiefs
over their faces meet some youths sho
uting and with guns in their hands tw
o girls run out yelling extremists in
losions of blind violence let's go th
rough the events of these last few mo
nths the months which led up to the c
razy morning yesterday began on Satur
over houses with the direct appropria
tion of goods although this proletari
an behavior is confused and disunite
d it goes towards expressing the refu
side the employees see guns pointing
at them and get pushed into the corri
dor in the room a meeting is going on
I heard confused bawling he said and
day 17 January in Piazza Duomo there
are the feminists their program is
to do it well there's room for them t
oo if they could possibly do it serio
sal of fixed wage-earning work and a
wish to reappropriate qualities in li
fe to affirm their own power in the
struggle towards communism they are
then I thought about closing the door

in the corridor I bumped into a numbe
r of very young people with their fac
es covered up and guns at the ready t
usly instead they want to go into the
Duomo the police however doesn't want
them to and the feminists ask for he
lp and get it since there's always so
part of an emerging mass charge of in
dividual fury for better living condi
tions young people who live in the gh
ettoes around Milan are left out of t
hey told me to get out straight away
threatening me at this point they beg
an to turn the desks and furniture ov
er and break the windows then they th
mebody ready to run and help the fem
inists what can't be understood is wh
y the help led to clashes in the cent
er a carpet shop being looted in Port
he metropolis and the affluent proces
s which they are however forced to wi
tness it's a young proletariat which
does not refuse to work if they can f
rew Molotov cocktails in nearly all t
he offices the flames spread quickly t
he raid lasted no more than five minu
tes the group then got away quickly b
a Vittoria windows smashed at the Fil
iadelfia night club and the finale of
the fascist hunt let's go on to 6 Feb
ruary general strike for four hours t
ind it but one condemned to wretchedl
y underpaid jobs the revolutionary le
ft has already grasped the meaning of
this element there is therefore reapp
efore the police arrived the fire bri
gade which had caused serious damage the
rooms were destroyed that evening in
he reason this time is clear Milan by
now is the industrial crisis capital
the 4,500 from Innocenti/Leyland risk
ending up on the streets dozens of fi
earing in the neurotic Milan a ne
w and very different image from that
of students with bags crowbars moloto
v cocktails left over from 1968 altho
a telephone kiosk near Porta Garibald
i Station a fly-sheet was found claim
ing that at 10.20 a.m. proletarian co
mbat groups occupied and destroyed th
rms are closing or are fighting for s
urvival less clear is what happens af
ter the incredibly ordered Trade Unio
n demonstration whistling and bricks
ugh they still exist what can happen

we must realize that these episodes o
f isolated violence express a very wid
espread violence a new 68 could come
e central tax office considered guilt
y of robbery in the eyes of the prole
tariat guilty of milking their income
the mobilization today during which t
against Storti Cisl then one of the g
roups heads for the Central Station t
akes over the building blocking railw
ay services for an hour reading of a
about not a student one but led by th
e young proletariat we shall see let
us look at other goings on in the out
skirts of the city and in the hinterl
he Confapi was also set on fire shows
the degree of development in the work
ing and proletarian avant-garde the h
eated message ended by saying that a
communiqué over the loudspeaker prop
osing to commander but by whom then
and with what prospects Innocenti in fa
and there exists an emarginated frust
rated mass of young people deprived b
oth of work and the very possibility
to use their own free time these youn
program of attack must be set again
st state economic and military terror
ism so as to build up armed proletari
an power at 10,05 the carabinieri stop
our days later Tuesday 10 February wi
th workers demonstrating but its a fu
ry without outlets groups of employee
s of firms in trouble burst in to the
g people are neither martians nor pro
vokers they come into town because th
ere's nothing in the suburbs they see
everything that they can neither have
ped the 61 bus in Corso Monforte on t
he bus a number of spanners sticks an
d crowbars thrown under the seats wer
e confiscated sure it would be easy e
head-quarters of the Regione Lombardi
a the regional Chairman Golfari is su
rrounded insults fly slaps in the fac
e the usual door-keeper or chauffeur
nor utilize and so they explode and t
here will always be these young peopl
he however a program of attack must
be set against state economic and mil
nough to explain away these events po
litically looking upon these episodes
of violence as underhand maneuvers b
y groups and attributing them with th
ends up in the middle he too one who

works in the evening the bulletins bu
t who benefits from the crisis there
will be somebody no one only learnt a
itary terrorism a program intended
to build up armed proletarian power b
y evening the tension had provoked a
new outbreak of violence the commando
e spreading growth of the city guerrilla w
ar fare however recoursing to tension
strategy is too easy an interpretatio
n which explains everything and expla
bout that episode the next day from t
he papers Sunday 22 February the scen
e is once again Piazza del Duomo the
cardinal is reading a homily on abort
s action in the morning had developed
over a wide area striking where it wa
s presumed the police couldn't interv
ene straight away in general they onl
ins nothing the first observation whi
ch comes to mind is that these groups
ion those from Re Nudo planned to stag
e people's festivities in Piazza dell
a Scala at the last moment permission
is refused and they go to Piazza Vetr
y lasted a few minutes and the chrono
logical account makes you think it wa
s a plan organized in the minutest de
tail the first action began in the ea
have their political motivation and a
lso their ideological background the
explosion of violence which we see be
fore us is not so much a spontaneous
a between Piazza della Scala and Piaz
za Vetra it seems that the shortest r
oute passes near the Duomo and then
the usual works spring into action ea
rly morning when the workers demonstr
ation marches were getting underway h
eading for Piazza del Duomo antiblack
leg groups made up according to the p
explosion but rather a channeled one
or one that tends to be channeled in
the form of political action and such
a process springs from a general situ
monstration police incidents but here
too there is something which is not q
uite clear cars are burnt riots again
st the Iran air company and the Banca
olice of elements from extreme leftis
t movements began to move with a fine
-toothcomb through small and medium s
ized firms around Milan the first ser
ation with respect to which the tradi
tional differences between proletaria

t and sub-proletariat between class i
ntegration in working-class environme
d'America e d'Italia and finally the
siege of the Church of San Lorenzo Su
nday 29 February at Bruzzano just out
side Milan a meeting about the housin
ious raid twenty or so young people w
ith handkerchiefs and balaclava helme
ts to cover their faces with molotov

cocktails and sticks burst into the t
g problem turns into a road block and
in disorder no damage apart from writ
ing on walls they are the graffiti of
the Milan gone wild anyone can go and

June 1976
(*English version by Clive Foster*)

Luigi Ballerini

FROM: *Che Figurato Muore*

in the shape of an unharmed almond, of a yelling sponge,
of a magnet dissolved in a bestiary, in the obscure
meanderings of a dagger, in the indolent eye of theft,
tongue of exile swarms against the wind.
You angle you wheel you cord of mirrors
you fortuneteller and you transvestite are in labor

★

and so crockery, licorice, swim,
so spine of an egg, so ambush,
and then a lamppost that nurses, fountain
of glue and blue puncture of cut,
and still this squatting of excess,
this pinocchio-kneecap inciting
the skimmed belly of your death,
on spread wings, steep in voice, in the void
of doubtful thoughts and reprisals,
of blowgun and fox. If it discolors
in a glove: the violet shell of sex,
the rent of the three of diamonds

★

here is the mute substance of path, cutting
not knowing, desolate cotton on a twig,
heart in suspense and wax of encumbrance,
and here's the arrow of the seam, pregnant,
uphill, here's the interrupted hostage, the fasting,
the mallow with feigned eyes. Here the Indian is defrocked,
theft adjacent, the variant thrust back in chimera

★

if an acute slowness were skin,
gusts of leaven mastiffs,
blue ointment of the rebound,
if one's face were white
and its color were to die in the leap,
o yes, exception, in wrinkle and nose,
in the diligence of song, in the sudden,
in fear that the unfillable distract
the ear from its swarming.
And often millstone of the everless and tail,
and opining variety of the hole

★

first dominates green, the hand without bird lime,
without a cap, the easygoing sand, the salt,
then the promiscuous tortoise, the indolent eye,
the microphone beating on the abdomen.
Last responds the woodworm, the doubled stakes,
the incessant gum, the finger dipped
in oil and albumen, wrapped in sugar paper,
nailed to the top of an apron.
If one wins it's by the roller of stayers
that swells and rots, that dyes
as refractory wool, as goose pimple

(tr. Thomas Harrison)

Dino Bedino

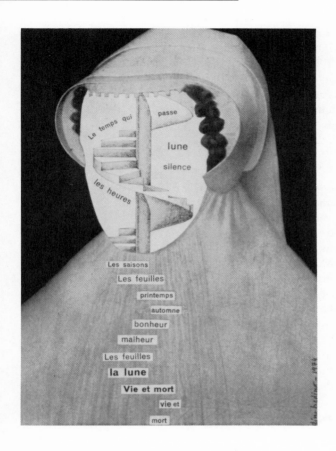

[*Elégie pour contrebasse et musique noire*]

Gianfranco Baruchello

Life to me seems more acceptable
if I'd expose myself right now
as an officer in the Red Army:
entering rest rooms
a glance in the mirror
would do. The black leathery busby
turned up at the ears
makes the red of the cloth
star stand out.
That's it
the eye tired with long duty
as a guard at Sinkiang,
the face of a fifty-year-old
who wasn't in time
for logistical reasons
to be on the Long March.
But even with defense units,
in the provincial brigades
there's a few crumbs of glory
and many reasons to go on.
Here the matter-of-fact
interest of those standing around,
the morning customers
of the café on Rue de la Cassette.

(*tr. Paul Vangelisti*)

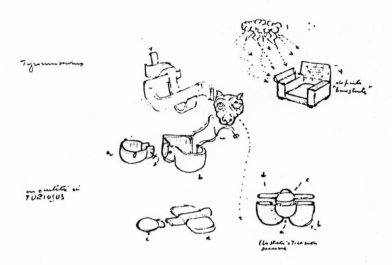

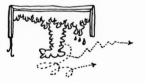

Franco Beltrametti

FROM: *Another earthquake*

---

imagine: incurable! a precise
sensation (not unpleasant – not pleasing)
          that everything is happening somewhere else
at the speed of light SVAAM   while here
24 hours in a flash or 6 months it was
                              the twisting road
up and down across the valley

3/31/70

? are you – seeking – something – in – hiding?
this is too much. where did you
find it. who gave it
to you. where did it
end.

---

or else :
like tripping a
centipede !

(a false move
is not permitted)   3/38/70

from a letter to Tim Longville (4/12/70)

No I have no greek theatre in my backyard
No I have no backyard
                    and shacks like mine
     is all I see
but it would not bother me in a garden with
     (every once in a while) a greek temple
in some far corner
     (out of sight)

                                   (*tr. Paul Vangelisti*)

Mirella Bentivoglio

Gianni Bertini

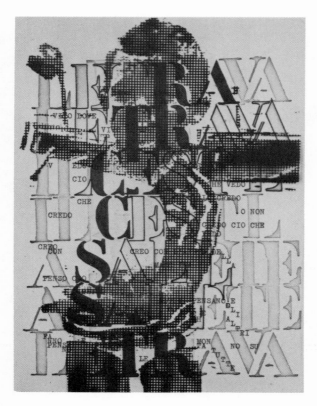

[*Le travail c'est le santé*]

Irma Blank

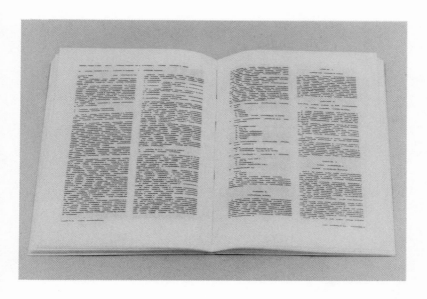

[*detail from Document abcd*]

Tomaso Binga

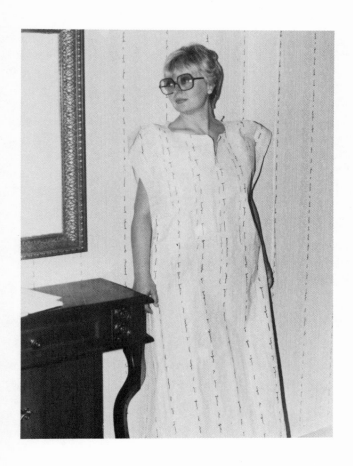

[*I am a piece of wallpaper*]

Edoardo Cacciatore

The Latest Lamp Posts

For sport, sex, crime with avid appetite
The readers unfold the popular magazine
Hold it the wrong way round tired of the right
In the end the larks turn into falcons, glean
The next sensation the fabric does not sway
A whirl of revolving legs desiring leers
Suddenly all of the world of today
Emerges from that morgue with myths and fears
Roll down the shutters what a deafening din
Vibration of the lamp post of modernity
People hurry to find redemption in
Work but are later corrupted by
      Bribes – the politicians smile and make a sign
      But reality expels them from its design

Solitude and Multitude

The cinema dawns phosphorescent
Messages of security
At the glass doors fires – a pharmaceutical
Sunrise in charge lies there in wait for you
The coils of smoke unscrew
Each one in turn – me, you

Come among the others take your place
This corridor is your passage way
Mechanical the toadlike voices leap
Resurrected sending up a hymn
Your frontier is the arm of your fauteuil
This is the El Dorado you enjoy

The others at your side in their divers' solitude
Bay is the dark or covering quilt
In a group amidst sharks and turtle-turning flights
Each one is stripped of guilt
Onan oh Genius loci
Sex and murder you nullify

Cautery of the senses and lava fighting ice
Fornix at the bottom of the echo
All ears all eyes the mind is quite untouched
Society a distant age
A dream whitehot like a blowtorch flame
As an accomplice presses and keeps watch

Love without backbone without even possessing
Is down the staircase hurled
Terror wipes the sponge across its snout
A sultry solidarity
There's shooting on the army range but still
Nobody can ever kill

Order reigns the patrols don't point their guns
Tyranny though in the cosmos
The truth however viewed and falsehood
Are the same thing anyhow
In the eardrum alternately
They create another eye

A single body with valves which laughs and pants
In a harmless catastrophe
The parallelogram knows for sure
A superficial diastole
The objects vehicles have become
A pearl is reason but a prickly one

One by one as outside the traffic swells
You solidify calm
There's less ice in the neoclassical
Which has the fire of bronze
With this emotional discharge
This, then, is how truth is dispatched

But that's no fiction what evicts dismay
O panegyrical membrane
The senses are captive time's undone
Genuine feeling collapses
Suddenly the dark is interrupted
Dismay again is erupting

Hands from their pockets take out their papers
Each has a screen as a reading desk
From heading to heading the plenipotentiaries
Draw with a leaden weight constraints
Subdued whispers blindly blandly
Offer conditional surrender

Over you, the others, draw the same cover
Hospitality is satisfied
The organic lesions the copious nudities
Make the viewer come and go
The fading has a nexus
You dream and dream and you are awake.

A City that Has What It Takes
(New York)

Beyond whipping rain and battling of eyelids
Constantly less and less memory is
A feast in the open – then of a sudden
You have the genuine city in fine weather
It throbs with iridescent lights beauty is to the fore
Ruthless free of lamenting

Among the banners in the wind there, where it undulates
The embroidered *Fight Cancer,* joyful vigor
Equips sibilants while the varied hum
Lends many colors to the breeze
And evil from hiding gives itself up
Innocuous now in those stripes

It sews compresses distances and the lips
Of nearby terror, which you avoid,
Trained up tools have and the dream is tested
Of being in real life with living people
The most insane image does not inspire nightmares
Rather health is global

People rack themselves for wages and the perfect circle
Of fines yields nothing gratis
Reduced to objects in clots of things
Already people take off at a tangent
This mad race crinkles the banners but vague
Certainty pays in full

Give back the change from this hollow exertion
Painful your approach is pounded
The very one who enjoyed the precise reward
Tastes the fruit of nothingness
The city lies around from its lights emerging
Your are a road and people cross it.

(*tr. John Cairncross*)

Nanni Cagnone

FROM: *What's Hecuba to Him or He to Hecuba?*

as the needle passes into the thumb
(is the somnambulist)
and
of course that time
is,
except myself

★   ★   ★

every ever furious children
play the times
(their hollow naturally)
while they grip the dead
by head and foot
they drag me

★   ★   ★

was swallowing time in entering the body
,
a thing shattered by agèd actors

★   ★   ★

in the diminutive of the tombstone
sees him wringing his hands
because sees him wringing his hands
(Baba the dung)

★   ★   ★

(the lowest ponderable)
a fact indifferent
that bought
the disconnected guilt of the consecutive
(the infinite mild impediment)

(*tr. David Verzoni*)

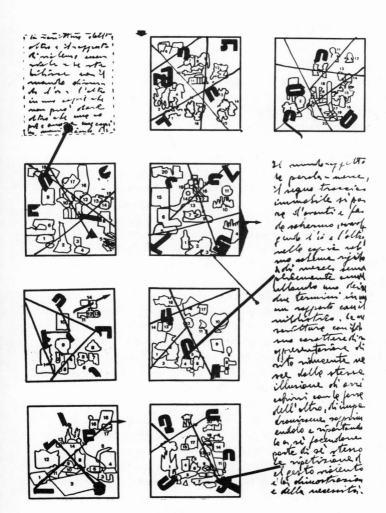

Giorgio Celli

FROM: *The Gothic Fish*

5

over the crumbly earth   over the waterbearing stratum   the seismo-
logical centers   the sudden telluric hebephrenias   and they flow
above the slate they run   over the feldspar they flow   germinating
the feldspar   the clay   the aqueous rhizomes that are petrified   by
shadowy caves full of algae   kinesthetic aesthetics   of the zoological
world   the arachnid   I know this is geotropic   negative: wreckages
  sometimes flint amigdale   radium   watches   for the eons   the
vortices of sand   within   the whirlpools of salt and ammonia   the
fauna of petroleum the landslides   of moraine amphitheatres
techtonics anticyclones exhaust the clouds   fallen straight down in the
quicksand   the carbonates that with carbon dioxide become soluble
dripping on the ulnas of skeletons   the alluvial eyes of the hominids
the roots of the convolvulus sprouting   in the orbit   of some anxious
catastrophic moon   germinating your opposable thumb   long hair
whetted like flint   pressing on the coccyx vertebrae taking the rood
through the diencephalon   I emerge   :   over all things the gothic
the anthill the pyramid the   labyrinth of Knossos the cell   petrified
the nuraghic construction the   trophophoric digs the fun   nel of the
trapdoor spider the pirate galleon   the exoduses of the peoples   the
biblical plague   of   the locusts (mandibles and tropics)   :   (where
man for some months ceased to pass)   the grass covered the bone
structure of the iron quaternary   the stinging nettle suffocates the
wheelisms   the roots perforated the lead tubing of the aqueducts the
der mestes opened galleries in the epidermises of the telephone cables
the   lichens sucked the black blood of the diluvian   cataracts the ter
mites pulverized the cadastral   maps the cer   tificates of good conduct
the   criminal records   a gracious octopus sucked Venus' rosy clitoris
who   was regressing into the sea   where man thought it possible to
return   the meadow saffron astralagus   the rose   under all things
:   the gothic

(*tr. Paul Vangelisti*)

Agostino Contò

FROM: *Oh, ah*

XI

if the plot, whose substance
we keep on reducing right down
to its very core,
doesn't reckon on trying to fill up
the page
the empty crazy whiteness

frightening and yet the emptiness
emptier remains
the belly of the full stop
is bloated or otherwise blows out
going back
when there's no fear at every step
                at any joke
of being knocked down
more jeered at than ripped off

and who's still afraid
some of those kids among the chestnut trees
the hilltop tower where the pine martens scurry
where the spooks dart about in the night

(oh the virgin girls,
entwined among the horses' tails!).

Corrado Costa

A fire that awaits the sun to get warm

there was at night beyond the confines of the fields

a   fire

one easily can see it was put out at night

all the fire there was was put out

it is   invisible

as one sees it

As if they did not know it

to speak e.g. of
leaves
they begin not to speak of
leaves
they speak e.g. of
colors
to speak e.g. of colors
they begin not to speak
they speak e.g. in
secret
they make up no names

to speak e.g. of
other
things
they don't
speak e.g. of
other
things
they speak e.g. of
nothing

One implies the other

"The happiness of living in a squash is insurmountable."
— Franco Beltrametti, *Nadamas*

but to live here where everything has been taken
is not comfortable or happy like in the grapes
the berries
happily or the tic tic
inside the empty zucchini or the falcon
in his feathers
to live where everything has been taken
is not comfortable we are face to face with nothing
before us
the void is so full
we cannot enter
but remain at the edge
where everything has been taken
and there is not the least
extremity
to stand on
if
everything has been taken
is not convenient to look inside
within the transparent
there is continually outside
to look that
has been taken
we stay outside
face down under the void that
lies face down
they have
taken
nothing
and you are afraid they will do him harm

They Go to See 3 Movies

1 : *'In terms of light'*

So then they make us continuously
watch movies
with actors who run faster
than the film.

The speed of the film is constant.
Occasionally we continue watching
movies
continuously at the same speed
with actors who are much slower
than the film.
We don't know
if we came in before
or after.

2: *I survive by a silk thread reminding me*
that the origin of human existence
is almost entirely based on nothing.

They even make us watch
an old Chinese movie.
The old Chinese movie lasts three days
and three nights.
We find ourselves on a desolate plain
where three armored horsemen
meet only by day
in pursuit
of three armored horsemen
who meet by night.

3: *'The Life of Lenin'*

With absolute fidelity
the real time
of Lenin's life
is respected.
Reproduced with absolute fidelity
the dreams and insomnia
of Lenin. The crucial moments
of childhood, the school
years, everything is repeated, even random
conversations at a bus stop.
The silences are respected. The lapses.
The movie lasts 54 years.
You should see it
at least twice.

(*tr. Paul Vangelisti*)

Maurizio Cucchi

"New Reasons"

1

The usual reasons are not enough.

To correct oneself, to be yourself and someone else,
to be in a thousand different places . . . sometimes still,
sometimes turning . . . coming and going: men.
Every unexpressed possibility . . .
To take part naturally, to join in with feeling.

You can't get any further,
blend with others.
To leave no stone unturned
(even now, lack
the soundest models).

2

(but who does the spectator's eye belong to?)

In black and white live forms, cold outlines, distinct.
Extraneousness without time. Scenes.
With the benefit of emptiness, omissions.
Mentally already at the height of the gamble
in narrower spaces: the bilberries, the cows,
the artificial lake, St. Brigida village.

Trivial illustrations. Cottages on hill-tops,
landscapes; and so on. Thumbing through the encyclopedia.
I meet all our friends,
acquaintances. Perhaps. They are doubles,
types. The program so accurate, elementary.
Absolute economy: precise, fanatic
in the calculus of probability.
Maybe the passion of long ago for sport,
geography.

3

The cobblestoned yard below,
where you didn't let me go.

Somebody I knew alone in the house
listening to 'Begin the Beguine'.

Over there people throw slippers at each other.

★　★　★

Frail, but smiling
if caught by the camera.
Very precise in his aim.
Difficulty at the beginning in forming my Ts.

However the smacks I got were unfair: infantile injustice.

(. . . standing on the table, all ears, obeying my father's
initiation in the rules of boxing,
la noble art: right, left, attack,
on guard, target . . .
The unequal challenge, but the winning knock-out, just.
. . .
. . .)
At last, dreaming, wishes and congratulations conferred
by pious professors.

★　★　★

You can see me I was
in the photos of my innocence.

4
. . . or let yourself go, confident at last,
to the warm softness of the bath water . . .

(I fear very much for my own body,
I fear my blood will suddenly gush from every orifice,
dismemberment . . .)

Anyway, completely whole: secretly hidden
in the womb, eavesdripping, in bed, in the heart
of the earth: sirens, crickets.
And yet something around me has happened: – shadows,
you say, you were asleep . . . Don't be silly: no cowardly trick,
but slimy, in vulnerable areas, inviting:
the fingernails, the fingertips, the intimate parts of the body.
In fact
now I'm alive, I talk as little
as possible, in milanese slang.

The trip continues or starts again,
who knows toward what future.

(*tr. Silvana Colonna*)

Michelangelo Coviello

April

Lascivious wrinkle face a vastest
or then roaring vice docile
ridiculous sound adolescent for
the dead because

      a real one kiss him but really real seen
      this and stricken hearts give us back our beauty
      her curled up between the thighs emptied out hold me
      the thing the soul learns where on the ground begging
      those hands and feet runs away from this : each his rest here
      in the swamp your friend covered with sand head torn to shreds

      her fat don't task me pardon an inexorable one
      I'll bite she screams atrociously though wet
      staying rapidly swills down playfully craps out
      very much! but pours forgets very much
      a whispering uncovered benevolent demolished

here! often open blessed ow
delicate break : groan : body!
and today after dark after joy and murmuring
o thence April

(tr. Paul Vangelisti)

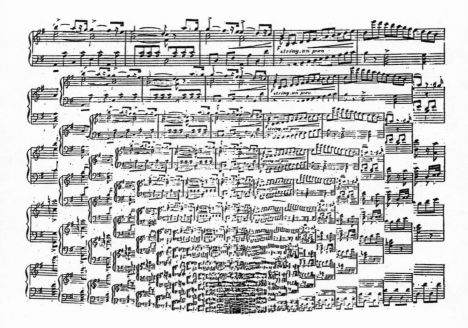

[*La stretta: a page of Donizetti*]

Milo De Angelis

I was offering oil for a golden flame

Brethren of the exploded universe, the eyes of the beast always betray: a random touch will reply, four arms to support a rose or to love the prophet who always comes to betray his disciples, weird brethren of water and circle, alphabet of flesh, pursuits:

There is an uncompromising wind which fells the wisteria and the branches of beseeching: now it's burning even its own ship, while the oarsmen's shouts seem to be the first prayer and the angel of God is a deep syllable. Kneeling, the lamb said: if you look at me, if you look at me in fullness, you will understand that there is no sacrifice ever!

There is no sacrifice. There is a stellar force that seizes the sickle and then reaps it, which pushes everything and each body towards another killing, that only body which the colt stupidly holds back from a deadly race. There is a first born word with no mask, and no one can flee into the following instant.

A spear slips into the wintry wheat and hits the fingers, now that the riddle returns to fairytale and rain on a game of hot potato, evermore unrelenting: lamps skirt the road, but she runs into poplarwood and fights a duel with every leaf, on equal terms, her challenge being bold.

Now! They are shouting, fighting, scratching a shadow, and their eyes are trembling nor do they recognize faces, spheres and planets: but the loudest scream of the mouse in the valley interrupts the battles, on the other side of that instant, and reveals the fresco and the cyclone.

And the deep time of the seed, it is singing, a flash on the rust again raging, while gravel whitens the sky and wheat ears cover pussy at corner.

Then children quench the thirst of the waves, blind the white demon, and sting the thorns, with the gay vengeance which hunts death, scratching its wings with nettles and making it then tumble down the nightly stair.

There is a secret, they say, there are blackviolet eyes, golden roads and long fingers chasing the galaxies, it's the secret of the sea oils, of the other breath: there is a black puma by the door, a murderous

claw in his eyes, he puts marble itself to flight and tears silky pass-
ages: beyond each tear there are lunar cities and birds of the abysses
with a breath which raises ditches in the air and gives to each hurri-
cane its rain.

(*tr. Antonio Mungai*)

Enzo Di Mauro

Easter (that Wednesday, the adjustment)

Drips from bright caverns of roses
the soul of the cat at midnight
while they play, they try to
shatter themselves, "Niobe (haughty memory
of nursery rhyme, tenuous pantomime)",
what useless streaks of honey scat
ter the lepers' hospital so the
generous magpie loves the betrayal
of the shingles.

The Flies' Place

> *J'ai fait un pacte avec
> la prostitution afin de semer
> le désordre dans les familles.*
>
> **LAUTREAMONT**

Each act if it escapes stripped
from the serene rubber masks
pestilent husks the circus smile
the room for the azure table companions
(or woody liana, secretions
of the she-wolf), it drinks during
the yielding obscene gesture Cornelia meanwhile
'til a newer effect turns up
in the house . . .

(*tr. Paul Vangelisti*)

Giuliano Della Casa

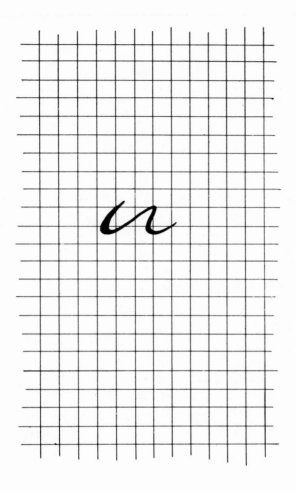

[FROM : *Alfabeto*]

Fabio Doplicher

Cage de Scene

gleaming with sweat we'll arrive
at the end of the show
shrieking to the shadows "now which face is mine?"
I've a photo with me
in my pocket some old memories
amulets of a past
which improves among the spider webs of a desert home.
the madman's tower
the mouth of Etna
German Empedocles you who didn't know the orange groves.
the revolution, the fire
the icy silence
of our motions
free in the illusion of verses and desires:
all is paid and all will be said
meanwhile our shoes crackle like bundles of sticks
the night watch is deaf
the boys have leaden eyes
the red bird took refuge
on the mast and sleeps after fishing.
might it be within a net, the choice
which will force us to measure the space
to recognize the man's membranes, the acid miseries
the lonely appointment that dooms us equally?
don't be startled, every folly
is a quiet lake
our angers rely on a narrow hollow
they are the small daughters, frothy in the first raiments
of the space which abandoned us.
then, the boys who seek the hate
with a sensual need
in the deep puddles of a sick summer
in the restless heat of the bricks
warmed by the sun from Mount Catria, in the exhausted outskirts
disfigured by her sons, the gypsy greets you
in her eyes a flash of a sullen pride,
I wonder if there is a need for hope
the masks hang in our hands.
yes, I lied
and still I will lie
and if nothing else is possible

I will paste on the memory of a love's afternoon
the second face which the warm rocking breeze
holds by a thread of skin.
the iron curtain is lowered
the wickets
isolate the place of the fires.
and yet here it's cold, the light is white
a thin dust from the golds and velvets. outside
the fire
from hand to hand
the torch from unknown man to unknown woman, anger and
        prophecy
and a need to curse.
because the ash is good – a girl tells me – the ash
frees the imagination from everything that it has been
and makes it up to me.
with how much toil
and secret disgust
we, apprentices of the art,
learned the rules of this theatre.
your hand is deep
to say goodbye and so long, like the sunset
and you laugh, maternal and ferocious, at the poet who makes houses
        in the trees.
all are dying, it's true,
the pines lose their needles, from the idea of beauty to a skeleton.
but today death holds no vigil over the forests from the towers
it lives its own metaphor
divides every other image within an immense darkness.
if this yoke is intelligence, body, sensations
if garbage and mud encrust the hands
and time recites trembling with delirium
and knocks at the iron door
to be heard, because it has been, "I existed"
he screams, "I, I" and only a smell of burning
answers him,
will we know how to invent
other hands, other hearts, in the blind race against the wall
where the wintry locust, lame of its color,
dreams of the air's snares, and bets with the cement
about its immobility until the next season?
the art of having to be; between the velvets of loves,
the continuous changes of scene,
and the bats from the sky which come here at sunset
as if to a large cave.

now, like crazed actors, we play
everyone with his own face
that one, precisely that one
which they told us was impossible to see from the dead.
and yet each one readily
identifies himself with that rigid muscle contraction
of the slow waning eyes in need of light.
it's the easiest part of the play
and we, impudent masks, didn't know it. time
seeks the trap door, it clings to the curtain, falls,
outcast angel. "the days won't be enough for you"
the prompter mumbles to me "learn the lines from your mask".

(tr. Luigi Fontanella & Judith Davies)

Flavio Ermini

rimini and usa

nutrix of the couple
lingual over glass
the oaks it occurred
burdened by the rapier

intact de chasse
that she to me be salt
ingenerates anger
by a worthy fandango

"panting she arrived"
twenty one people
dwelling . . .

(tr. Peter Carravetta)

Gilberto Finzi

The Cost of Life

a game reserve, opportune
moments in open space

> you can easily read the contact with the
> devil

vomit filthy lies spitting excrement
shells fossils enormous dinosaurs tattooed

> on the back – muscles – on the
> p-a-t-h-w-a-y

> the unpackable packed

> happenings strength court of arms

now

regarding the Cost of

(this diagnosis

> suggestive – frenetic – passive)

> the temptation (just as in the : of the : for the)
> (very latest years of history)

> infantile mythology

> money glory success

> > (italics in the passage)
> > a happening (or happening ?)

Fear Nonsense Weakness

> really for well-being ?
> > (wild oh fleeing geese)

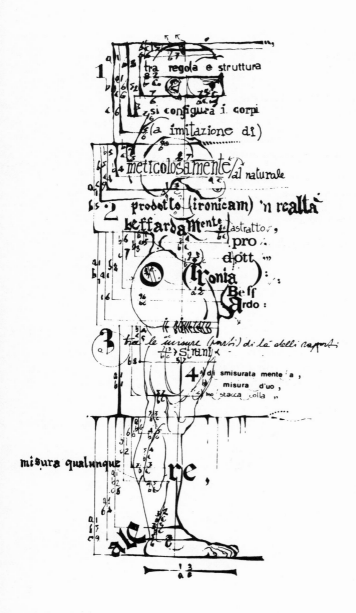

[*Tra regola e struttura*]

Luigi Fontanella

A Little More Paranoid

to Gianfranco Baruchello

come on, open the door
and the blue and pink circles
    SUDDENLY
more light less light,
how much chatter in the kitchen
"I made this for my
Be e etty" he said dangling
his arms long long
his black mouth gaping;
"there are too many ants
in this house" said the other
and by then his hands touched the
floor. Muzio entered
in a wheel chair
and already the instruments
had begun to sing in the kitchen
    OPEN STAGE
vapors, puffs, pistons, pops,
pans dancing boiling plates flying,
and Muzio with his whip
now here now there, there here there
liquids in ascension
DRINK! (Edward, one of the first)
"but I", "drink!"
how nice it is to go for a buggy ride★
and desperate races along the pines
of Cinecittà at 5 thirty
in the a.m., I AM THE WIND
Arthur A, arthur – who is it? who is it?
: Eddy Hyspaniel, open
the door I tell you, would
you open this door, but BUT
how many and WHO will be on the other side?
Remember Barbusse who wrote
a novel on this idea,
then the studies the interpretations
the interpolations, the extrapolations
the essays the discourses the dissertations
the congresses, conventions, anniversaries,
saying: the transfiguration of one's own

autobiography, extraordinary invention
always goes well on the dustcover
ZUBBINMÈTA ZUBBINMÈTA

(tr. the author)

★In the original: *harrozzella*, which means *carrozzella* in Florentine dialect.

Biancamaria Frabotta

Penis Envy

cosmos shifting momentary illuminations
roams the philological impulse of a star meets
the propitious ritual of your curls kissing

early morning hours split into two halves
the apple of the first-birth dream to the Martian angel
who kicks teeth nails in the stratosphere

I extend the mercy of a lily worn into stone
filth-picking in February nests decrepit birds
in squadrille tumbling headlong dropping motherhood shit

verbal predicates gothic bedsores (from the points)
the dream skids spaceless through the female fir tips
ice-cold sharp angles of the North Star

it was an adolescence of identity death
I'm ready to wager your coveted brush
egg-bearer for alms who blooms dissociate Twins

sneaking away on constellations of slander
uncertain I play you stubborn lose myself decapitate capital letters
tracing a metaphoric asthma I pray for you no play

seduced I'm abandoned the old song sung
at Sanremo a spiral of skylight and of windows It is
scientifically proven that tube contractions can be
spastic.

(tr. Keala Jewell)

Alfredo Giuliani

FROM: *The Tautophone*

i myself and the theater

in long times of silence i stretch out under wide canopies
        of backstairs
or i perch think of those clever cavaliers
        riding
their foul wolf to the dancing school was always a blessing
        for me if i seek to understand
what i think weave the fingers stretch out elbows
        and thumbs

in fact she explains the rabbit cloak on the grass shaggy
        as you what sweet
pelvic pulsations when she raises knee and finds
        the snail the body is all
in natural grandeur which proceeds as in dream the move
        ments slow in the plasma
i don't shut my eyes arms in driving position on
        a flaming truck

tuna looks up between edges of scarlet sage it's
        green-blue as chinese
turnip and must have hidden significance for us if
        pavement is black glass
and tapered girls in unknown city further
        themselves grope raising
huge bubbles of soft perfume from beneath moon gleam and
        also stumble

there are those that dance on glass surface of stream i see
        delicate embroidery
of the footsteps the forest wheeze and army of muscle
        without knowing why
porters handy umbrellas on the spine till a group
        of exiles in flight
fake relief of daily tension in the howl of wolf
        they inhabit

now if i seek to understand the precision of troubling waves
of the still body
of the tiger killed or stunned among bushes i
don't allow third eye
to excite my brow anus could ache of itself to the point
that i believe theater
work of mystery and applause imagined by men and
intelligent beasts will rise again

Then the experience happens

if you want a little lead well here it is if it happens to you one pole's
enough to move the chenille
mat to the right with one foot at four one speaks with haste
in the corridor
the cat on the sidewalk below is no longer discernable
this is a monstrous city
where the armpits of stores lift seaward i
understood it from the first moment
strewing gray pins packed in the eyes of aging
girl in the rose air
of a room without paying attention to the hedge
shivering on the moquette

they hook her nose quivering under trousers on the curve ready
to pull the break or cough
and then with nothing else to do except talk excited of crackling
anarchies and inhale
the ecstasy of the operator it was a good job sunk
in another's coat collar the nails
at the window fade on newspaper master of life outlines
of sensibility hinder us
appearances of exploitation revolving chair carries
havoc of escape inside
the monumental immersion will not get higher to tell us
likewise it isn't down in sand

(tr. David Holzapfel)

Milli Graffi

"*Kreuza*"

       To get up.
Kreuza
       didn't lift the blankets.
Didn't lean on her elbow.
Didn't stretch her back.
Didn't put her legs out
       of the bed toward the
       floor on the rug the
       feet and first opened
       her eyes to get up.
       To get up.
Kreuza
       changed the definitions
       of horizontal
       positions.

            (*tr. Paul Vangelisti*)

Giuliano Gramigna

"*La Main Gantée de L'Assassin*"

1 : Not dragons chimeras a machine made of teeth
    Roussel the bottle of mineral water ;

2 : not : the negativity of language before again
    that of shapes invented by the light
    of the courtyard on the wet glass in the place of decency ;

3 : horror/decor of language from language descended from the
    branches of that bourgeois ;
    the other should be pietas–obscenity of the sign glosseme

4 : saying the thing in the sign not blind the sign echo
    echolalia abstract sign full of its abstractions
    like the red and blue of the pencil

5 : etc.

6 : Surging where surging not the pernicious mushroom
    of buttresses capsizings Velascas
    because the evil is not in the world
    but elsewhere in the diencephalon that stupefies and splinters
    its wheelisms a membrane tom-tom
    softened by the sudamina

7 : and going out in the sun that dazzles (plagiarism)
    the light of the pre-post squall doesn't dazzle
    roulant the bus its length far away
    mirrors of shards of mints luminous with towers in the sky
    gray limpid squared;

8 : and within chaos the blessed citizen and bay-windows to flight of
            stores
    unrequited spaces between Jezebel and Formalhaut (*) THE NAKED
    RUNNER ((*) I created confusion Gentlemen I should have said
    between Achernar and Deneb or the Pneumatic Machine
    or between thumbs and index fingers mouth and anus poetry and
            non-poetry
    between not and not);

9 : horrable unhorrable – but what
    language am I speaking? –
    thoughts of death the very
    tranquil melancholic distant nonmind
    all those things that were past and present
    in the center three hundred meters at the bottom of a lateral
    (which? sought supposed burned on the map of the city)
    near via Visconti di Modrone;

10 : desunt aliquot alia in this type of collage
    and the vice of pieces is its truth
    and like the vice that shatters

    from shards of luminous mints of the mines
    of Falun (and the hand with the glove
    and this excess of copulation;
    the vice of pieces that shatter
    for a clearer reconstruction a

demoniacal clearer in its pieces
separate from his thoughts of death
in his forty-eighth year of age
(WITHOUT LEAVING A TRACE!) and too much space
passes between one atom and the other improbable the clinamen
of age (48 years) not epicurean.

11: The assassin in the taxi carries the gloves
instructed by the système Bertillon.

(*tr. Paul Vangelisti*)

Massimo Gualtieri

Fauna of the Eye

Cancelled difficult to explain
passes across the eye
as in the shut room
gurgling the crank
in the dusty stratum
natural metamorphoses the anomaly
of each little word
distanced from the word
already pronounced
and better the dream than the reality
the mechanical sleep
of red cadmium and yellow
in ironic simulation
coal coal
fauna of the eye
in the sign already seen.

(*tr. Paul Vangelisti*)

Giuseppe Guglielmi

Décuplage 11

1

Once that that happened
                          when you speak softly
the original face the blood
                          whatever thing opposes
now joined through the movement
                          fearing that nobody saw you
the ground is blocked by your feet
                          la peur à oublier ses doigts
à perdre ses yeux now he's alone
                          only a thing of wood and zinc

2

When you speak softly
                          I held her delicately in my arms
economic relations are impersonal
                          they represent themselves in this form
the power to take it out of his hands
                          fantasy is essentially regressive
it exists only in an abstract sense
                          when body and mind
whatever thing opposes
                          my ego from a long time ago

3

Beats his marble of black letters
                          it's only a rose
it's still a movement
                          he believed in the existence of something
but once that that happened
                          the silence involves him
his birth was the decline
                          leave that those who don't know it
show proof of it
                          spinning on a high wire

4

Whatever thing opposes
                          that it was done to give background
economic relations are impersonal

just with him who seeks

his rigid identification

    with the toothache and the rest

un arbre élu par l'orage the neurotic value

    today he seeks only to breathe

we were all a little while in Eccles Street

    the dialectic with which we demolish

5

To write not writing

    the ordered conceptions crumble

gloomy shouted lazy

    an inconclusive stutter

of splendid senselessness

    it's more than a simple parody

instinctively avoiding language

    it's not a complete affliction

covered with illegible writing

    travel with no point of arrival

6

All night so tranquil

    not wanting to mix

the sudden vision

    the internal conditions

they represent the most extreme form

    on lacquered vases for export at a good price

I dissolved in hot water and sugar

    from the turbine of the world

the subject of much sentimental foolishness

    the language of defecation

7

The folly of searching

    that which is never lost

the urgent desire to save oneself

    every attempt to grasp

it's only a strategem

    can't call himself empty or not empty

once again that doesn't mean anything

    he'll seek to escape

a manifestation of grasping

    a deceitful resemblance nothing more

that we have explained here

(tr. Paul Vangelisti)

Tomaso Kemeny

Inclined Plane   (1974)

boojum – all the scomforts
stay here in europe with your tits
to the others the bass drum (of) "I ain't there"
listen to the concentric circles of (the) directrices
: (cool it, babe) : "freddo chirp chirp think it over"
(((((they guide you)))))
hairy nonachilles
poisoned notbycoke
and do pretend to enjoy yourself

it crumbles dense (endos)mose
denatured but the mafia ha-has no outline
with pins it croaks shadow of scraper-smog
and the linen maids' march ha-has the upper hand
but the metatarsusmattress creaks
effraction without a chaste idler

he toasted some spittle (on his brow)
he stood soma and zanathos (on the conjunctiva)
he bent his hindquarters
he repented ("feeling surrounded")
(neither he unlaced his boss' eye
nor the avalanche of vaginas nimble a trobar
nor the unshorn in pompibus
nor with jaws buried alive)
he dishooded and unbeckled neglected

(tr. the author)

Giulio Leoni

The High Madrigals

I

alas, the act of knowing you: form of a conventional progression of the
    heart,
frequent outrage for who feels you palpitating (for me, ergo; with my
    cool pain,
interwoven of clear poetic art, antistrophes, epicedia about me, aulic
    verses:
I, the auctor, stay in these broken logical figures, as: You exist → I live);
alas, the act that you interpret as confounded folly of sequences,
    reducing action
V exasperation of chains, tight by ourselves in love of forms, in bonded
composition: (Gestalt-solidarity of affections, ritual actions
laid down in a geometry of gestures, allusions to our passion:
and explicit declarations, invocations, also)

II

thus a catalogue of our enthymeme, in the anomalous, unlimited course
of our 'ergo' (graphic image of a possibility, idea of the system of being
V act of creating a logical form in this 'in der Welt sein'), while
we're composing a death cantata, or receding now in the schema
of a theory based on 'you' (monema that actualizes your absence,
makes you a figure in a bounded space, dejected from the profundity
of a group of atrocities: (you) (real phenomenon, unique concrete
    being)
(also staying uncontrolled factor of a divagation concerning the
    universe,
metrical element in a farewell address)

(tr. Edgar Vincenzi)

Arrigo Lora-Totino

FROM : *Testo Seriale* (chapter xxv-c)

bou the

ger

and

in

fou sin

it no of our ter

abbess all by I is say there

a at being either now or shalt taking
thou to venial were will

whatever casuist quoth under they nor only
mortal distress turning betwixt yourself as amicably
further confessor are into then all
slightest convent halved like together
least another division sins leaving from thus
hundred any half rest halving then alternately
my dear person becomes diluted off
more pitch course times see giving accordingly
turpitude pronouncing therefore
syllable fa sol la re mi ut continued
matins vespers complines come
daughter andoüillets set
note saying

```
ring     ing                                    w
ring     ing                                    i
ring     ing                                    n
ring     ing                                    g
ring     ing                                    s
springsprings p r i n g springspring
sproutsproutsspprriinngssproutsprout
springsprings p r i n g springspring
sproutsproutsspprriinngssproutsprout
springsprings p r i n g springspring
sproutsproutsspprriinngssproutsprout
springsprings p r i n g springspring
sproutsproutsspprriinngssproutsprout
springsprings p r i n g springspring
sproutsproutsspprriinngssproutsprout
springsprings p r i n g springspring
sproutsproutsspprriinngssproutsprout
springsprings p r i n g springspring
sproutsproutsspprriinngssproutsprout
springsprings p r i n g springspring
sproutsproutsspprriinngssproutsprout
springsprings p r i n g springspring
sproutsproutsspprriinngssproutsprout
springsprings p r i n g springspring
sproutsproutsspprriinngssproutsprout
springsprings p r i n g springspring
sproutsproutsspprriinngssproutsprout
springsprings p r i n g springspring
g                               ring     ing
n                               ring     ing
i                               ring     ing
w                               ring     ing
s                               ring     ing
```

Nino Majellaro

Knowledge of Things

for Pia

I

The water that beats down with the persistence of a metronome
and makes dough of the houses is like the daily paper, it's a sodden
idea that our minds can be purged
                                              of prejudices.
there's no lift away from a direction
the aim, or the end, or another direction
are mercifully hidden from man, there's no way
of checking how many dead stand-in for our death
and a subjective probability can't remove the error.
Others decide beforehand what we will taste at table
and guesses words memory shifts are a wall
that it's just as well to verify if we want the day to match
facts: you can be insane and get to know it
from others.
                    Behind those overseas provincial tundras
that are Valàssina camp in palaeoanthropic solitude
Maroccans and prostitutes a season is relived here at the level
of the encephalon proving that man does not perish
                                              but what's the use of that?
once a man's got to the station he's no longer the same man as left
so that they can't exchange destinations
like a purely combinatorial mental category the future
we haven't lived isn't ours nor is the obituary notice
after our death between dream illusions and reality possible remains
        with distractions
terrors in a theatrical performance where the space doesn't match
the character who may have come from Venus or elsewhere
                        at the supermarket the volume of the goods being
represented by the price every article with its price stamped on not easy
to put one over on "them" everyone has the price he's worth stamped on him
some call it destiny others class death.
Is the hero who died before the revolution nameless? for the future
it's not expected conditions will be different from the present ones seeing that
other brainwaves are unlikely

2

with gold prices going up the advantages of
a good collection of writings to look after the emotional involvement of 30,000
readers what is it we call logic?
what really happened and how this stands in relation to what we wanted
to happen? between one and the other thing "the military" featureless
        a man who died after the revolution
didn't happen could be left his place of death
where he is or will be recognized as a revolutionary without power
doomed to decimation ten fragments of a thing finished
without being known, killed without having killed
        would visitors go where there weren't
collected bones and fancies with papers of men
not adjudicated by the productive cycle
                eminent?
history makes visible dignified men anyone who has ever fallen off
the winged horse has been crossed out in the gods' primer!
To contradict the compendiums of bourgeois mythology
you must die with your back
to the sun's path and not make an elegy out of death
nameless but efficient trash but cumbersome proof
against today's weather and rusted before "they"
can organize space graves free of the inertia of semantic
interpretations before they have changed all the signs
a determined man has no choice he can make except that of class
he has no other choices he can make
              freedom nil.
While one evening I saw my father's death throes move through our galaxy
and trees warm a motionless December
now if I look for an explanation a few quite useless memories remain
you don't notice the important things in time in the intervals
a mutation occurring in the chimpanzee doesn't do man any good
and vice versa when the species are fully established
the genetic links between them snap and each goes
on its way and I collect sequences that no one can piece together
perhaps just an aesthetic *collage*   poetic strivings in search
of meanings even if weaker and more relevant to the subject

3

is the nostalgia in which nature and presumption merge
and which by destroying them provides a safe refuge for rejected ideas.
        The growth of a planet outlives thought
and what outlives thought
and knowledge of the world finds a spot even where there are no alternatives

to the life of a plant
             the landscape not being entirely made up of words yet
or entirely of things   is almost a sedimentary aquarium
of fossils in chains turned upright
if the act of poetry is deceit there is the deceit
of the universe in every star seeing that in every negation is present affirmation
I can see the point of light go by/and the silence behind it in search of a space
in this horizontal ladder.
             And so we have the illusion of words
words before in some way or other we slide underground
as dead men or as survivors man chimpanzee gorilla contemporaries
as reproductively isolated species
and the common ancestor belonged for certain to a different species
from the three
             we have made man with so little effort
because to decode delta and theta rhythms in cerebral currents
to vanish through hybridization to be men is one of many ways in survival.
So many unexplored silences in our bodies
every one of our bodies' silences unknown to the surgeon
who only know that of the tumor and only when
it's visible our thinking is like the surgeon's hand
when he's found what interests him he leaves the rest to the sharks
the poor man knows revolt and desperation this is the price he pays
to find out how hard it is to find out the catalogue you're supposed to die in
because not even the things we got to know
spring the meaning of spring youth
have a continuous sign confused by the different interpretations
of meanings and each interpretation an erasure
we decided what end to hold the rifle by
because every interpretation robs us of a hope

      4
either you reach some destination or other or you give up
and to communicate between dead and live men back–dating every year
algebraic negative sign we would reach life so as not to have
the concept of life
             everything we know
contains not what we wanted to know about it
but what it itself knows concepts structure
memory and a familiar landscape consists in perceptible lines
everything else becomes blurred as though we've left it without interest
alphabets made into a future
             By means of philosophies
of economic booms I have lived my only

space-time durationless life I've lasted long enough
to feel myself unable to last any longer in the future
they have drawn military boundaries that between illusory
and possible not even the mind can get out from *homo homini lupus*
how sweet and storybook-like Hobbes's slogan seems
tested on millions of men per year the river
flows into the sea so as not to become a river the river-dweller trying
to resist with freedom of speech the freedom of man
just as the birds that were once fish did and moving
around our impossible picture
                            the knowledge of things being
shorter-lived than man he can't know himself
man except out of fear
                    the seagulls come and go on behalf
of travel agencies, will we have to die without anyone
seeing it? between dark and dawn; by the shortest routes; it's better
to follow the suggested itineraries where you're sure to have
what you need even after you're dead
                    the law of increasing entropy is still in force
a non-Petrarchan triumph of death for material forces
for mental forces the law of finalistic evolution
and so the triumph of life
                            "history is bondage
                            history is freedom"
freedom knows nothing but laws
armies level freedom
slowly individual reason is extinguished

5
Everyone is a firing squad's target.

                                    (*tr. Evelyn Bradshaw*)

Lucia Marcucci

Angelo Maugeri

FROM: *Dis/appearance Record*

★ ★ ★

the movements of being better between sleeps
here's the episodic start blocked by the compass
the alibi to avoid the focus of forward escapes
the trap of shades opening the dances

★ ★ ★

a mistake is the sign that multiplies the total end
constantly increasing after a phrase the arrest
blocked in a leftover card living on robbery
a no-matter-what object easily impressed

★ ★ ★

the broken stiffness of amphibian copulation
l'allure décontractée of the coming summer
all that was changing shape sowing
hair unpricking the curly back

★ ★ ★

because arrest is the sign that easily multiplies
after a one-too-much step the end of every mistake
blocked in a no-matter-what object living on robbery
impressed in a card constantly increasing

★ ★ ★

in a computer forecast by the machine
it does make sense to see the little games swallowed
an image multiplied added divided subtracted
all there is of one's own re-impression

★ ★ ★

because the total end is a sign multiplying
a one-too-much object in a no-matter-what mistake increasing
easily a card scored after the stop living
on robbery impressed and constantly paralyzed

★ ★ ★

they stand up to shout behind the ones that are looking
farther away from here where they fall full of stings
working on the bottom where they are shot because in the night
they stand up to look behind the shoulders of the criers

    ★   ★   ★

the obscenity of un-laddered mouth substituted
for tight-body-belts a new suppleness
of tongue shocking pink worm/whored
the loose stocking is the beginning of touch

    ★   ★   ★

the slow burning of the fuse the extension
of the ignition of the unquenched iron of the starting handle
with abandoned shoulders the shirt shapes
putting on shirts on shirts large sleeves

    ★   ★   ★

at the elbow wine nuances lips & moustaches
painted on doors it is here rubber tubes erect
cracked balloons sweet crêpe for the girl
fresh in themes and colors because he told her

    ★   ★   ★

listen it is really you white-striped and with collar
against the linen twilled-cloth T-shirt
soft refined sensuous the one that goes
looking for the mouthscene a return to the norm

(tr. Angela & Carla Locatelli)

Stelio Martini

Qui se souvient encore de sa jeunesse

sans en sortir brutalement *par des jeux* boursouflés *doute de sa vocation*

car les sujets possèdent ce qu'on appelle la guerre et
l'adieu .

Six rêves dissemblables (format de poche) convergent vers une destination
secrète

Je voudrais mourir vite et être un gentil spécimen dans la glace.

Mais *Voici quelques suggestions* aux jambes lourdes : le mourir en scène, s'il vous plai
et

l'espèce humaine qui, devant des mots qui ont étonn

démesure son tintamarre. *A*ussi le despote le plus éclairé

regarde du coté de *six âges différents* qu'effraient le
progrès.

Mais la vie n'est que la clé sous la porte. Des centaines de trains n'auraient pas à
faire un beau cadavre.

J'ai cru un moment que mes mètres attendaient tout ce que j'ai découvert.

Il faut tirer comme si l'homme ne « voulait » rien savoir sur la mer et pourtant

TOUT ça C'EST BON POUR LES GOGOS ■

[*Schemi*]

Eugenio Miccini

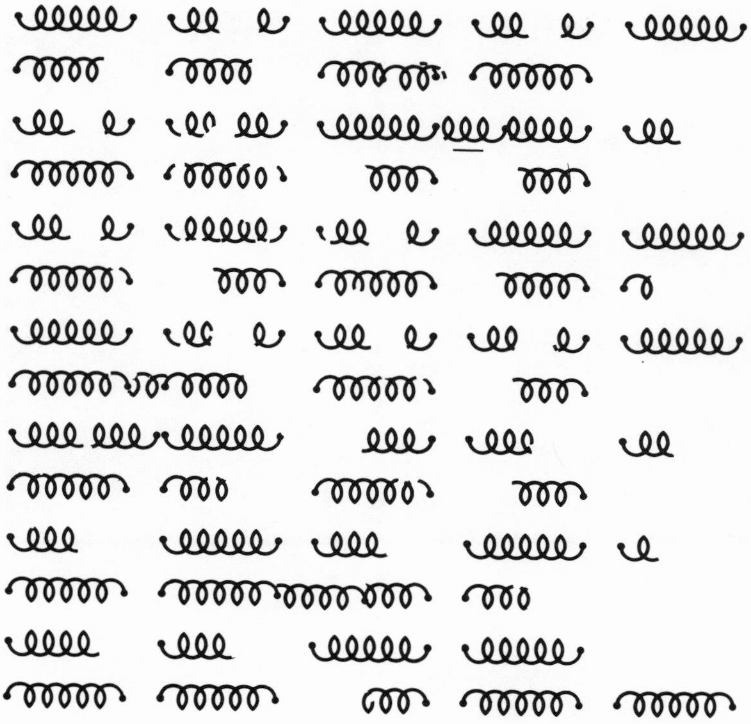

[*The Blunt*]

Maurizio Nannucci

Giulia Niccolai

FROM: *Substitution*

The subject is the language

An idea of vengeance: the retaliation
or revenge of the word which has been thought
(make the gesture of inventing language
perform the act by which you appropriate language).

Though dependent or superimposed
the individual and the word exist as separate objects:
not a mutual agreement of words and things
but the pleasure of interfering.

Things exist to be said
and language narrates. It outrages in turn
a language already violated by others
to possess language is a way of being.

The subject is therefore the language
with which to commit a capital offense.

Syntactic and verbal

A careful and syntactic space
plots the fraud of today's findings:
it makes itself impractical
absolutely careless and random.

Objects and events in the imagination
the suitable matter found in the texts
acquires a clear and precise tension
a dreadful will to think.

Scattering fragments and clippings
in a sort of slow dissolve
it collides with the framework of the text
(a result of its own process)

Obviously one cannot say
it continually seeks to destroy itself.

(tr. Giulia Niccolai & Paul Vangelisti)

E. V. Ballad

(to Emilio Villa)

Evening and the everest
ist vers la poetry leaning er
isst er rit er tells a tale
des bear's der splash! mit cul poilu
nell'acqua bass um la forelle
zu farla saltar fuori
to make the trout jump out.
Puis il se lève la trota nella paw
und isst und rit und ist der dichter
every very big indeed so froh
und bär so rare und weiter.
Ça au national park
But all america la calzi
come un guanto zeus rabelais
il t'amusait ce luna-park
you fed computers coded data
coddled eggs cod-fish balls
un cassoulet la fricassée
un potage dame edmée des côtes
de porc grand-mère les couilles
du père and out came brunt
H ha quel frisson quel high-toned test
quel high-speed text
tapiocal un bel incest
er mejo the best.
Off frisco uper the bay
when rose fingere'd dawn
shone forth that day nach
dem orkan dem hurrican
su quella piramide di phoques
(es war phil hip that west coast mentor
qui me l'a dit)
you saw nausicaa and like a mountain lion
dal fitto groviglio dei rami you broke
a spray
athena auch war da she touched your hair
in a certain way shed grace
and combed it col pettinino azzurro.
Ma sul canto sesto there's nothing more
to say.
Ich wollte ganz for ever
once and for all

à la manière de *ev*
von *ev* erzahlen et
sinon la *v* qui est si
véri table eventuell
evidenziar la *e*.

(*Febbraio 1975*)

[*Sculpture*]

Martino Oberto

[*Journal Anaphilosophicus*]

Piera Oppezzo

Disequilibrium

All of our life
shivers in time because
of unbalances and expectations,
of acts impersonal and unconquerable
in their abstract expansion.

Each day
circumscribed by time.
A present, external time
which we follow aimlessly,
our spirit a little destroyed
by a natural inclination
and a logical consequence.

Consent

In our space (we) always fully present
unsubjugated by memories
unbroken by tension

tragedy can occur
if by a connection of facts it happens
it will overwhelm us wholly
whole we consent to everything.

We could have been happy
we are sure to be happy
beyond our expectations even though briefly

because reality
can exceed any image
and in all of its moments
show us a synthesis.

(tr. Luciano Martinengo)

Luciano Ori

inno al sole / hymn to the sun

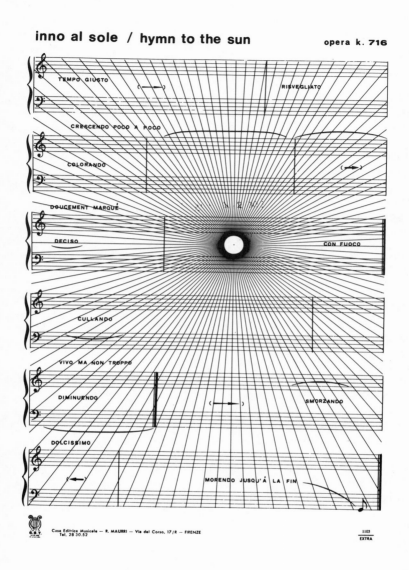

Elio Pagliarani

Objects and arguments for a desperation

to Alfredo Giuliani

What do we today, poet, know
of our death, private?
                         Poet is a word I seldom
use, but here it's necessary because
once every type of priest has been repelled from counseling us isn't it
    the poets' turn to speak
of our death, now, to illuminate us about death?
                                              You
corresponded when you said in those lines
that I suffered and I had a prideful vertigo, fearing adolescently
not being able to die. Or believing.

                         I pause
I reread this opening it's not bad I rub my hands
where I have a little seasonal rheumatism, I remove my glasses
I look at my eye in the mirror. I don't understand, I can't judge
but I know that doctors check the eyes, I don't know if mine
is turbid or dilated or protruding, whatever can it mean: I know that
    now my neck
muscles are tight that writing this note
will keep me very excited that I'd say it was worth it if I knew
that within three nights I'd get back my sleep rhythm.
                                              Alfredo and I ask
around various friends how's my face, its color.
                                     Even you
that same adolescent thought, even you
blanch sometimes suddenly after a meal.

There are no immortals in the streets
they told us that mankind, not a man, survives
that for us it's the same immortality as beasts
in reproductive love, and if I knew or not that it was
the only act permitted beyond the limits of oneself
the necessary homage to the rules of the species
even I felt myself in a great natural rhythm
on top of a woman and a sea was watching us
as if we had a purpose, or we watched a sea
as if it had a purpose.

But this is what distinguishes man and the wager
here's a phrase invented by the elite, in any case it's true that some
wager on never dying.
                              Pride is needed: to believe
that the work itself the pen not us but the model itself is useful
to others; faith: that history
pays on time; etc.: and the wonderful thing is that from this wager
the only one to have no proof if his works survive him
if only for a moon
is the one who wagers, who dies.

                                   I told her, the same year
I knew the stimulus of sex I translated a sonnet of Shakespeare's
badly, "Shall I compare thee to a summer's day?"
between 1939–40, with the ending
"my verse will live as long as men
know how to breathe and you with it."
                                   And you with it
woman's face, are you now final?
                                   And now concluding
the breath that the clause fulfills
resolutely?
                 I traveled far and wide
to forget her, in twelve hours near
her face in the heat
opened itself in an easy sweetness
but from me poured out only
the bad faith of the intestines
                              in bile and excrement
and the panic after, and the clinical abstraction.

And the physicist with the cancer in his knee, with a cow's knee
what screams, hit there one would've told the fascist, hit him in the
      knee he's got cancer.

How many alibis now for not loving
                                   and she insists on the phone
if it's this in me that interests you, I add that he's in Bologna
that at this point they'll amputate his leg.

                              From some time I no longer
exalt in the adventures of the spirit, for some time that which burns

it just devastates me and I can't go on
making poems on my skin, to sublimate
my defeats, to presume signifying

me and her and the penultimate explosions
$$\qquad\qquad\qquad\qquad\text{to draw a moral}$$
of universal death to console ourselves from our own.

But if I'd only cursed
now Brecht has already left said to your children
forgive us ourselves for our own time.

(tr. Paul Vangelisti)

Anna Oberto

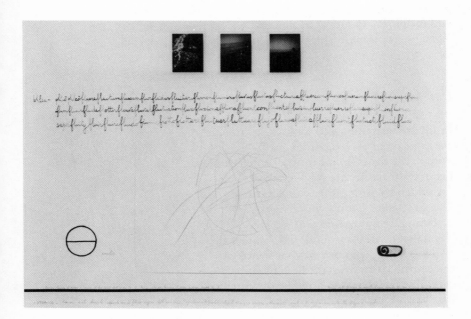

[*L'Utopico: Eanan e il tensile rapporto
con il flusso magico dell'universo*]

Renzo Paris

For R.

If anxiety is such that filling yourself with pills has no longer the
      physiognomy
of a game; if I arrest myself looking at my faded
hair and a penis that shrivels and gets up
after repeated short circuits, who should I thank?
It's hard to swallow this dust,
to think of that sharp-eyed old man stepped out
of a fable not ugly or beautiful or even too pious.
Nine years are a lot, like the saints of long ago
and the flaming wheels of my infantile tortures
and the ninety spouts of a fountain.
Even poetry is no longer the same.

For E.P.

From the beginning you look like a little girl,
the same one I played doctor
with in the fields, in the most obscene games.
From what family are we? – I asked you,
forbidden by your pleas for protection
"on all levels." Didn't we even visit
a young director to find you work?
Then that confession about the hammer that
you weren't able to use on your fiancé. And
the earrings torn from the flesh of your
ears. I've said that you could be the sister
that I never had. So why am I dying to touch
your cheeks? You have the eyes of a sphinx, and besides
you're a lesbian, you never stop telling me of your love
for this well-endowed woman with a thousand appointments.
You have the name of a fable that I've never understood.
You're shrewd, I've got you. You treat me like a brother
suddenly found in a city full of surprises.

                              (*tr. Paul Vangelisti*)

Claudio Parmiggiani

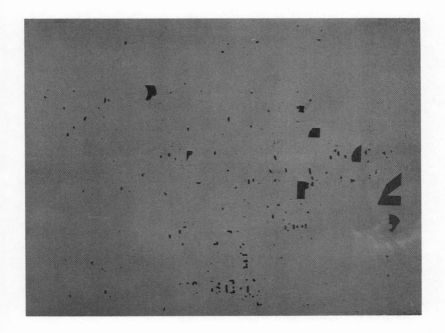

[*Found poem*]

Lamberto Pignotti

"New York Refused to Produce Disasters"

He seeks in every way to escape,
To break the barriers of his existence,
but wherever he turns he sees nothing but anonymity and
habit.
He goes in search of new land and new seas:
Television cameras were ready to rush to the
places of possible disaster in New York
and it is not the fault of American media
if just then in those seventeen-and-a-half minutes
New York refused to produce disasters.
It would upset the representation of a reality
that could be called frozen
immutable notwithstanding every effort,
widening the prospectives and prolonging them
to infinity.
Born this way
in opposition to this
is a world in which the habitual conventions are
eliminated.
At such results one can arrive only by putting together
fragments of men with things lacking any ordinary
meaning,
Tacking them together with scraps of sackcloth
with patches of red and black which emphasize the
unpleasantness,
almost tragic,
of the hemp and the ragged jute, moldy, run through
with holes and burns.
With this hue blends perfectly
the beige you will select for accessories.

(*tr. Catherine Suppan*)

[*Tutto scintilla*]

Raffaele Perrotta

FROM: *The Sacrifice of the God Toth*

And *this* writing of mine liquefies at the locus of congealing. By inscribing itself, it melts away. The Anatomy of the Immortal Language: words and letters being dis-seminated, letters that arrange themselves into words, words that arrange themselves into phrases. Great Mother Church falls, the Part For The Whole falls, and petty little churches and particulae are left to consolidate the old pact of the Accord. A heart alone, courage alone. But *this* writing burns. Sure, it has no *style,* it has no linearity. It abandons itself to the impetus of a Language not yet apportioned into National Languages, in juridical patterns-of-speech. *Burned Earth* leave *this* writing rent. Thirst. *This* writing feels the burning once again. And it doesn't deliver but the delivery of the Sign that ornamented Academy learned to take seriously: Heraclites' *semainein* not at all *localized.* From place to place*, I, tireless librarian, have a right to err. Errant – running, running-through running-over running-by – I *can* err. It's in my power. It's my possibility. The librarian goes through the loci† of the Text, and he quotes: but not to terrorize. The librarian is terrorized by the Library, by the same running-by of *this* writing. Understanding that does not understand, knowledge that does not know. The sight is shielded by the appearance of appearing.

*original has *l(u)ogo* ("place") from which the author extracts *logos*
†again, the original is *l(u)oghi*

FROM: *Sonatasituation*

for whom that country path?
the earth is neither mine nor yours
the earth is an ourness
(forbidden to forbid, like this May's twenty years)
and of ourness is thought

the stars sink their teeth into the gulls
   the carnationbelly (of my woman)
     the beaches
       the gates that open to the mornings

the knife of night holds up stages
   carcasses of nightingales

on the olive trees we've spread parched leaves
    nailed keys of pulp
        masks with fingers and no hands

we dry our hair

the ear stops at every corner
    gigantic ear

the telephones tell us our pockets go
sauntering breathlessly among the owls of ancient deflowered
    enthusiasms

(tr. Peter Carravetta)

Giancarlo Pontiggia

The Gift, the Branch

(for C.)

Look at the moment
that you leave on the tree,

the hare barely noticed
he is seen, like a step

as we go toward the snow,
this is the wind and the house

is blindfolded. But come and carried
by the wind is who watches,

meanwhile a winter returns
the other song of prey, and called

this is the prelude to snow, but come
as a foot to another. Beyond the moment

is this moment within,
here's the footprint watched and investigated

from below is eternity,
and the trap won't be light

from the grass, this step
is a step that nails down,

voice that slices the hare,
wind.

The shores descend ripe, but it's night
and loved by the wind descend to this

estuary wounded by time, and here
is the book of fire, when it is throat and they speak

in the rhymes of time,
but they sleep, and look . . . it's now, and it's a gift

and sea, and the gift of the sea is this,
to return calm, as when in the poem a white

search for waves and ships, and they look
at the serene she-bears of the sea, it's night and they look

this escape sought by the wind, and the story
is this beginning, when it is said

who is bestowed from the tranquil waters
of the lakes, and this is the bath

of the light she-bears, water and lonely nights
in the lake where the grass grows to song

and along here is this lóve, this steep
growth of the lake.

The idea of thunder and the white
pupils of the goddess walk
on the roads trampled
by celestial bestiaries, and they eat
(pour), shove the black
light of the hands which they
bestowed, and they say that the liquid lance
of maggots doesn't sleep, and he doesn't
leave the tremendous
loved one, whom a lightning bolt consumes in the lotus for

ever.

                    (*tr. Paul Vangelisti*)

Antonio Porta

To Open

1

Nothing behind the door, behind the curtain,
the fingerprint stuck on the wall, under it,
the car, the window, it stops, behind the curtain,
a wind that shakes it, a more obscure
stain on the black ceiling, a handprint,
he leaned on rising, nothing, pressing,
a silk handkerchief, the lamp swings,
a knot, the light, ink-spot,
on the floor, above the curtain, the scouring pad,
on the floor drops of sweat, rising,
the stain won't rub out, behind the curtain,
the black silk of the handkerchief, shines on the ceiling,
the hand comes to rest, the fire of the hand,
a silk knot on the armchair, it shines,
wounded, by a nail, blood on the wall,
the handkerchief's silk waves a hand.

2

She slips on the stockings, black, and slips them off, with her teeth,
the splits, the double-somersault, in an instant, the tights,
backwards, caper, then the splits, the breasts
push on the floor, behind the hair, behind the door,
it's not there, there's the backward somersault, the seams,
the handprint, backwards, on the ceiling,
the wheel, of legs and arms, sideways,
of breasts, the eyes, white, against the ceiling,
behind the door, silk stockings hanging, the caper.

3

Because the curtain flutters, it rises,
the wind, the light in the fissure, the dark,
behind the curtain there is, the night, the day,
boats in the canals, in bunches, the smooth canals,
they sail, loaded with sand, under the bridges,
it's morning, the iron steps, oars and motors,
the steps on the sand, the wind on the sand,
the curtains float their edges, because it's night,
day of wind, of rain on the sea,
the sea behind the door, the curtain fills with sand,
with stockings, with rain, hanging, stained with blood.

4

The point, the high window, there was wind,
he got up slowly, screeches, in an instant,
oval, a hole in the wall, with the hand,
in shatters, the glass oval, on the leaves,
it's night, morning, crowded, dense, clear,
of sand, of diamond, he runs on the beach,
got up and running, the hand pressed, a long time
motionless, against the window, the forehead, upon,
the glass upon the morning, he presses, obscure,
the hand sun deep, in the earth, in the glass, in the belly,
the forehead of glass, clouds of sand,
in the curtain, lacerated belly, behind the door.

5

Wheel of legs, the canvas slaps in the wind,
that man, his legs follow the course,
the rope coils, toward the breakwater, on the sand,
on the nets, drying, the cloth shoes,
the cement breakwater, they break into a run,
there's nothing but sea, always darker, the cement
in the curtain, slipped off the stockings with her teeth,
the point, has compressed an instant, a long time,
stockings stretched out on the water, on the belly.

6

Over there, he squeezes the knob, towards,
there's none, neither certainty, nor exit, on the wall,
the ear, then to open, an uncertainty, doesn't open,
answer, the keys between the fingers, the belly open,
hand on the belly, trembles on the leaves,
rushing, across the sand, the point of the blade,
the son, under the desk, sleeps in the room.

7

The body on the rock, the blind eye, the sun,
the wall, was sleeping, head on the book, the night on the sea,
behind the window the birds, the sun in the curtain,
the eye even darker, the cut in the belly, under the fingerprint,
behind the curtain, the end, to open, in the wall,
a hole, belly dissected, the door shut,
the door opens, it shuts, belly compressed,
that opens, wall, night, door.

(*trans. Paul Vangelisti*)

The Crimes of Poetry

1

she wants to be kissed on the cheek
meanwhile the blade traces a garden

belly covered with alphabet signs
tender queen in clogs

behind a hedge the cock
presses hard once against the flies
but is unreleased

2

thigh muscles with no trace of tiredness
regenerated in the act of consumption
blood machine
his body's triumph
grizzled tire skin

pump suddenly blocked at the edge of a stream
season erased and can't repeat
idiotic memory

3

entrusted to the care of an ambulance
finite waiting

as answer to an inviting cry
an even quicker escape

inert the open zips
the secret desire to kiss a singer
precocious inclination
hare in lettuce furrows

the holiday starts in the ambulance

4

you can tell a madman right away
in winter light clothing dogless
bed sores
opens his mouth spits a bit of bread

beats the sidewalk sniffs at cars
the breeze freezes his wispy hair his nose
a net trap now awaits the worn out man
who disappeared by chance they say

5

the journey starts tomorrow
after skidding on the snow
they finish up in each other's hands
then a good sleep

the sea slopes down to the horizon
there's a brisk wind on the marsh
the market shows up crossing a bridge
vanishes behind an opening door

6

in the park with the wheelchair
suffocating under the pillow

embracing her with his feet
clean where you sit

greets her and hugs her
quick smile forces him

hangs his hands on the tree
there's room for all the dogs

7

in the mouth a finger dips
tiredness gets up tomorrow

keeps the body near
I eat the life I gave you

standing in the hot-house which stains
a feather floats among droppings

flashes on refuse at sunset
I rot the food you ask for

(*tr. Loraine Willis*)

Mario Ramous

White Noise 64513

seeping
          voice from *white noise*:
that blinds you; take no hint:
your color only

                    fear
fllung to edge of curve

is already a progress,
                              nerve-holding:
not before

                    perceptible, *a capella*
it was a link also
                    sinusoid

to say it again is no more convincing,
that is within you: to drop it into the slot-machine

an escape
          a platitude
to be expected by repetition
of elements, a played-off ball,

it doesn't untie the knot: the next curve
has a different tension

                              daily sounds
a deceit, an addition
                              but the sun
a remarkable
          axiom

                    the flus, "now",
the irreversible flux of time   not
to be calculated by lack of statistics

what is in time be sure it isn't time

peering at the pouring out of fear

                    (*tr. Alfredo Rizzardi*)

Vittorio Reta

"My new address is"

my new address is
faraway lands Post Office
                    Sing to me again
                              Baby
        or just c/o Goto
                    ile d'amour
                              cine Champo lion
(and I think back) les images of the sixties all super civilized
poetry more for surviving than for writing
more for saying than
more for   than

just open this door – you'll find a packet of visas
and Mohammed that time in the Bronx(z) por favor
la luz in (?) camas
esta muy bieca
                nuages d'ammoniaca
like sleep I look for words
                        (describing that night by memory
                              the hotel hall)
                    when it began to snow
you started to give yourself a fix, the snow started to burn
my moistened eyebrows,
the blue lights of Bologna station and the hospital Avenida Luz
                                        London – darkest Africa
                              chuck out the old stuff
I possess identity cards that I'll put under the pillow
with this memory my viscoid feet avoid the spikes
                        I shout my head off between the sheets
I get up from this oval lake in which I'd fallen asleep
a wood was closing me in and the space restricts
                        the horizon contracts
              the image that was finally outmoded perhaps, in order
with her hands on her temples flagellating veins
                        her thighs from behind are like thrown knives
(I spat in the toilet so as not to throw up all the salt
I bunged up the night's snares with handkerchiefs)
which I threw in the Tevere along with the counterfeit passports,
passport stamps on cigarette packets,
                              passport stamps even on your forehead
                        on your wrist
                              on the soles of your feet

climbing down the trees   lifting every time   the elbows   over her
at times in her flowering fur coat
                        the head faded
and the day after I telephoned the victims
futile resistance they replied into the invisible wires
to gain time I did some sewing around her fingerprint,
in the silence which is donned like a fur coat
on the way to the border there is always
Tanger de mort.

Franco Rella

FROM: *Presumed Negation*

    4
Then the wind, through the desert, the houses
the trees, the roads, blowing, the desert
walking, watching
                    "those fingers touched the
pages on which my shame"
some shady lineaments, signs, a lay-out, a
crossing, dazzling, fragments, fault, a
fracture
        a stranger body, laid down, a fearing
evidence, grazing, remembering

the stretched hands, stiffen hands
                    lookin' for   thing

    5
And the proliferation of voices, things, words,
streets, square, houses, hooters,
walking, running, trees, acting, fighting

"to find somewhere, in the dark and contradic-
tory framework of facts, the way, the certain-
ty of a fact, of a thing, of a set of events"

in place of the crime
                 a fragmentation
still investigating.

                    (*tr. A. Chili*)

Giovanna Sandri

From K to S Ark of the Asymmetric

once it was

thanks   to   a   swarthy   wine
the waves
are
breaking
more
look   gently
there's the band
of a barrel
once   it was
full
of

they answered him water

awesome
as Orestes
the spring of
beauty spurts
(not to astonish
with its strength)

which robe will it be for me?
they answered him   water
the threshold and the step
kissed his foot

(*tr. Faust Paulussi*)

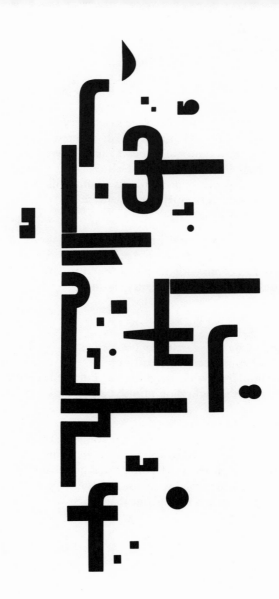

[FROM : *Uomo / o il Tempo*]

Amelia Rosselli

FROM: *War Variations*

In the lethargy that followed the machinery of
the few, I lay about, happy and disordered, disordered
to the extreme; and the tongues of serpents rushed
like fire close to the bolster. Close to the bolster
a dragon was dying, salami vendor with his salamis, his
tails that hung that hung very smelly, but delicate
in their scent altogether.

And if the antigone who awoke silently, very silently
toward my landholdings my disordered products, unadorned
with glory, if she had come with her pleasing scream
of alarm, I would have died, very silently alarm.

★   ★   ★

Fascinated by the practicality I observed a
usual man without curves carrying easily a rosy
mattress on his shoulders, while laughing like Pulcinella I remembered
you were there. And the night didn't finish badly, if it wasn't that you
      existed
apart from every reflection, and beyond every expectation. Returned
home after many and many a luminous sign you were there again
and again and again. Anchored to you your image in me
does not dissolve, you protect it: the image that dissolved
days and days and days returned with you, without you
for you in the solitude of this springtime that floats
in full winter, my soul!

(*tr. Paul Vangelisti*)

Edoardo Sanguineti

FROM: *Wirrwarr*

1

what could I do or say, Vasko, when that serious technicolor
Shirley Temple caught up with me running on the Lijnbaan, waving
her red tail, laughing? I suddenly felt her talons – as
one says – in my heart:
                              she holds my skull in her claws, but her face,
is clean, now: and she sucks my back-bone over this desert
of Rotterdam, inside this Number One, during this literary supper:
something (she) like Holbein d.J. (I'm thinking of the *Portret*
van een onbekende vrouw): she has not come out as well, of course, but
she is thinner: and with the bat on her head, for instance: and without
      all that yellow veil:
I even asked her her name (you heard it too): a word like Inneke,
I think:
            and now, what can I write, now, if I still have to discuss
until six in the morning, room 348, with the European Tchicaya,
with Breyten, with you?
                              (I am not even able to call my wife, see, to finish
Affinità elettive): and I also have a couple of pimples on my face:

2

it was the black man from Unesco, limping over the wide sidewalk,
      who said,
in front of the Atlanta (while we were laughing, desperately, by
      ourselves):
we are all roosters, we (the men, god's male children):
                              and he
crowed (boisterous Jannings, in the cold light of dawn), and
he gurgled, effeminate (for them, for the chicks, for the women):
                              but the (concrète-(German)-
Swiss (who has entertained senator Montale, in a villa of his at Ascona):
      who usually
lives in a small town near Nürnberg): (who works for TV and for
a china industry): (who prudently changed his florins, before leaving):
this concrète-(German)-Swiss, now then, dressed in white, who writes
      poems
about colors: about red (rouge): maybe even about blue, but
I am not so sure any more:
                              this concrète-(German)-Swiss, who collects
                              Vasarely,

said, then: but women, here (in Holland): but here they look at foreigners,
with interest: (and I said: so much the better):
                                        so, we immediately tried
with a sort of blonde Mangano waitress, while I was paying for the coffee
and the tonic water:
                        a non-polyglot enough chicken, though, alas,
for that incredible aubade of ours à la *De toren van Babel*:

3
at 6:15 PM Vasko calls me: are you awake? he says: sure, I say: and
I have already talked with my wife: (so the telegram was completely
        useless):
(but it does not matter, obviously):
                                        and I have already written today's
        second poem
(today, June 3):
                        good, says Vasko: but this is really holy
week, then, for you: (this one: of the Knaak-Poetry):

4
dear wife, I sent Cathy the postcard, with an urban
landscape (and the houses all lit up, well, obviously): and with the
        words: "I got here
too late":
                even the Turkish photographer signed it, who came
from Amsterdam (and sweats terribly):
                                        and I signed Sade, like I always do:
and now, guess who was at the Burgmeester's, for the reception (at 5
        PM at the
Town Hall): why yes, Leslie A. Fiedler, the one of *Love and Death*: he
        recommended
a novel, by a certain Hélène: (I have already forgotten the title): (but I
        have written it down,
somewhere):
                        and then, guess what was written (in the restaurant toilet)
again, it was really written, like this: "haben sie nichts liegen lassen"?

5
where are the forty poets, Tadeusz said (but maybe it was
Yehuda, who was talking): the forty poets that one never meets? (and
        will save poetry):
and where are the four poets, struck to death by a flaming sword
of whisky: the four locked up at B.M. Scheffers, all together (or in
        another restaurant
of the neighborhood), for a little bridge of words?

and what leuga was it,
if it was born without your eyes, without your gums? (and there was
    not even a dolle
Mina whatever, to put there in the middle like so: so as to copy her,
    like so: with words
precisely):
    but I copy your body, now, as I saw it in my dream,
last night: I copy it with these words:
               avec ces petites proses en poème:

                    (*tr. Giulia Niccolai*)

Aldo Selleri

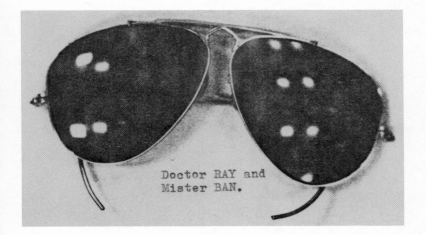

Doctor RAY and
Mister BAN.

Sarenco

[*Omaggio alla poesia*]

Gregorio Scalise

FROM: *Signs*

(. . .)
It's easy to think that the light
is an expedient.
But the trees must grow.
If only there were a space.

(. . .)
Memory under our skins places
our story:
one soon learns that each thing
is ruthless, if it is reduced
to the fading of the signs.

(. . .)
Fantasy no longer gives
space to space, names to names.

(. . .)
But to start again at a sign.
In the night, for instance, I extracted from a stone
the idea.

(. . .)
I would like to have again the biological fragments
of the house where I have spent the existence.

(. . .)
The nothingness becomes scenery.

(. . .)
But for the ambushes of madness,
I have to admit that everything is without sense.
I go where the cold is coldest.
The child in the corner, the wolf.
The evening falls, opens a world,
it doesn't mean that it isn't real.

(. . .)
An alibi moves the armies, the
stolen things.

(. . .)
The foundations crossed by spaces
render unarmed the essence of fear:

among wet flowers
the mind dispels the monstrous,
for the refined inhabitants there is
the exercise of life.
The universe renders each thing exact.
Useless to terrorize the mind,
signs of hazard furrow the wind.
People sit in the shadow:
but conscience learns what it can
bear: a free spring has flowered,
and it is evidence not to use
a man.

(. . .)
I would never have thought
that the world was always the same.

(. . .)

Carlo Sitta

Action

it starts the day before till late at night
after a long sleep restoring
the hour thick with rust scribbles on windowpanes

the next day from the first hours struck
after midnight till day break
red and green asleep halfway through waiting

you place the situation in a testtube you bring it back again
in trajectory in the circuit of tension   *for Claudio Parmiggiani*
the gesture doesn't budge from the sitting man

with the ingredients within reach in
daylight it confirms the version of the fact
he who remains loses himself incorporeal there is no interference

choose a formula from the book of social
ethics and give it life by any means
poisoned beauty seaquake on a nail

with the means you have at hand you know the osmosis
the offer conveyed on awakening
you enjoy an agreement of sand a scorching flight

choose any thesis from the codes and apply it   *for Claude Courtot*
immediately there where you are
the event retraces the absence shattering space

in the conditions in which as a rule you find yourself
always accept the version of the facts
the void doesn't knock at the door it whirls motionless

perform the slice in the book plough the pages
cross the destinies of the sign open the gate
the seed gets extinguished in the psalms it dies in the shape of a crystal

break down to molecules the decrees the law   *for Giuseppe Chiari*
fragments blown away by a breath on the palm
evidence is nourished listening releases voices

follow the unexpected plan you find before you
throw over your shoulder
the horizon dies in gold two steps away from home

anticipate the scene the lock which snaps
adopt your role interpret the grass the road
a program standing on stilts a honed delight

dress your distraction in years
within imposed limits on top of the rubble
the verification weighs the lens at the tip of exile

discover your negation the presence which burns
the session is only an open chapter
slight surprise in the shadow of the explosion

your presence persists in the shape of a cell
a chapter open to the anaesthetic rain   *for Maurizio Nannucci*
the outside doesn't burn color is spectrum

remember the attrition of bodies the equilibrium
broken speech conducted on a biological thread
in whirlpools of mud the circular door closes itself

reproduce your microcosm the inertia
of matter in the corner where a planet rolls
the secluded summit of ivory mirrors craters

(*tr. Giulia Niccolai*)

Adriano Spatola

The Next Sickness

1

consider first of all the position of things
eaten and worn away by time by boredom by cold
corruption is this hope that one reads in the eye
wide open and lost in the corroded bathroom mirror
in front of the interminable catalog of falling to pieces
within the intricate tissue of hours from midnight to midnight
in the company of a clepsydra of a cassandra of a catalepsy

2

consider first of all the position of things
the common cold the saw mill that screeches in your ears
the syllabic din of water from the faucet
the presence and absence short of breath the digestion
the odor of a wet body is synonymous with perversion
or excessive prudence or a spark in the retina
something beats on the temples we must open the head

3

consider first of all the position of things
you have become cordial you're not lamenting you smile
behind the house grass begins to grow
with its sweet lice green from green grass
this itching that you scratch is called spring
goldsmith and acidic salty silver and clay
be careful of draughts of the heart of one's thought

4

consider first of all the position of things
years follow upon years the question is resolved
by the maniacal obsession by the kitchen calendar
by the wind by resentment is lymph or tree bark
is trigonometrical breathing subdued polygamy
with the yellow pollen the yellow fecundity
thud of the piston bitterness antidotal

5

consider first of all the position of things
now it's not worth the effort to stick out your tongue
your suspicion is monotonous in need of company

there are chairs and sofas there is erosion of the wall
that leaves powder and chalky fossilized crumbs
pecked from the starving room gnashing with rain
the suitcase has closed itself the key has got lost

6

consider first of all the position of things
remove fat from the butchered meat the main course the microcosm
that fortifies the overly polite fortress the deaf insolence
the precision of the cut of the sickness of the garden
holly geranium snail centipede
this is what's called taking a trip
nature is stupid and good nature is evil

The Abolition of Reality

Georges Seurat
A Sunday Afternoon on the Island
of Grande Jatte (1884–85)

The wonder the sense of lacquered objects
bolted measured made up in the clock
generous happy mature penance shadow
the sun disbanded sews on the leaves
trousers hair parasols and gowns and gloves
anger drowns sighing the groan resounds
against the wall decorated and empty against the scale
gurgle unraveled dry enameled gongorism
congenital with thirst with gloomy astonishment
or wonder or the sense of lacquered objects.

[*A Sort of Caption*]

Preserved saved the black and white part
the pure orchestration the place for formulas
luminous lunar vibrations corroded
by the already said the already seen the exquisite lure
open upsidedown a sense of relation
between barrier and barrier between similar urgencies
without an apparent outlet without conversation
audible inaudible instrument of nature.

Fly Hunter

Loathsome would be the conception of loam
rusty spots on spotted skin
stillness of the hand poised on an old bundle
abandoned for some time in the square's angle
in Aristotelian perspective not too distant
from the perfect concept of geometry or the impertinence
of the eye of the flies flying about the room
phosphorescent around the landing strip
loathsome it would be to slay them without a strong grip

(tr. Paul Vangelisti)

[*Zeroglifico*]

Paolo Valesio

Performance

I don't know, maybe you're right about the intonations:
    she had the wrong intonations; and, when she burst into
that long laughter at the beginning, her laughter was wrong
    (but listen, excuse me, but how can one laugh right?).
However, when she let the egg fall
    which splashed over the white rag on the border
    of the area covered with sawdust,
    and some black matter squirted out of it (slush?
Or shit? No, it did not smell; mud, then),
    I liked it;
but then, you wrinkle your nose when I say so.
    And you explain:
    that she was too expressive (the traditional style)
    that it was not a really new show because there was
too much literature in it, too much (yeecch!) Freudianism,
that it was not a truly
    (many here say pérformance, with the stress on the
first syllable)
    experimental performance.
But what about the director of that actress (who looked
a little like her pimp, her maquereau),
    who the following day explained it was all based
on the concept of trompe-l'œil?
    (To be sure, he was a sophisticated fellow; who, in
order to illustrate what he had wanted to do with that
"Portrait of an Actress" – that was the title –
had a whole story ready:
    about a fictional painting set within a fake painting,
and then there is a real easel in front of a false door,
    and a submarine sandwich on the easel;
and all this, introduced by a statement of mock modesty:
    "I will be country simple").
In the ensuing debate a critic had recalled
    that the black egg is an alchemic symbol
    (but a symbol of what? If memory serves, the *chemeia*
is the art or science of black soil);
    Oh, what a disdainful smile did you have when I dared
to unsheathe, by this quote, such a rusty allegorical sword!

Well, to be frank, I liked that performance;
how can I put it in a better way?
I was convinced, I found it a real experience
("It's a real experience," say travel agents when they try
to sell somebody a trip to the Seychelles or some such
place).
In short, let's ditch the terminology:
I liked it;
even when she plays the role of the Classical-Romantic
Actress
hopping up and down as if she were on stilts and sum-
moning up a non-existent:
"Romeo, Romeo!"
then cutting it up:
"Meo, Meo!".
Well, I liked it, I (used to say as a child) leyked it.
I leyked it, my Darling with the Green Eyes (with
which I – interjection – in-oculated myself);
even when (above all when) you become ruby-red, because
of the wine or of a slight cold.
Shall we leave together, heading for Rome?
Okay, okay, I was just kidding;
I didn't mean to sacrifice your personality, deny your pro-
fessionalism.
Don't you see? I am listening to you with an enraptured,
deep-as-water attention; a feminine attention
(and while thus listening, my face acquires a serious
expression, my cheeks hollow out, I become demure – so
demure that I can't stand myself).
I listen while you explain that performance to me:
too expressive, too derivative,
with erratic and erroneous intonations.
And yet I would have liked
(but I hesitated and lost my chance)
to respond with some general remarks. As for instance:
since radicalism is, unavoidably, a philosophical at-
titude,
any kind of merely formal radicalism is a bad imitation
which risks becoming a caricature.
The mere existence of form
(this is what tradition tirelessly reminds us of,
this is why we cannot help but listen to it)
is the result of a compromise;
isn't it grotesque, then, to pretend to radicalize a compromise?

The limit, therefore, of post-avantgarde:
it is not
(as petty bourgeois folklore would have it)
obscurity.
On the contrary, (post-)avantgarde stumbles on its anxiety
to make explicit
        precipitously and simplistically
certain conflicts in the mind
and in society, and in culture
which require a more sustained reflection.
Now, such a reflection is often –
        unfairly –
scorned as academic.
And just what do you mean by academic?
Have a look at yourselves!
At your constant tendency toward vulgarization.
But you virago, you
you are so independent so detached that
when you asked me
        (heavy eyelids, voice slightly ironical):
"You teach at the university, don't you?"
        I – it was not your ironical tone, that did
not matter at all –
        I felt for an instant my heart in my throat
and frantically thought:
        And now, how do I hold her attention
for some minutes more, what do I tell her?
Something nice, I don't know, something brilliant:
or should I try for a show of culture?
        Noo, a resonant inanity is better;
better to divert the course of the conversation but all the
while holding to the reins of her horse, so that she does
not leave me:
        "Yes I teach, that's right; but now I write, I
do writerly research do you want some wine shall I bring
you the salt?"
        But, I leyked that performance.

                              (*tr. the author*)

Franco Verdi

Sebastiano Vassalli

Behind the Page

a sea of ambiguity
behind the page
　　—Nanni Balestrini

Behind this page the emptiness of things
The surfaces of words by now hide nothing
A whirlpool separates things from terms that designate them
this page is an immense shroud

ᵀ Jnder this page there's neither ambiguity nor history
Only blind violence and unnamable abstractions
The emptiness swarms with these larvae of words and unknowns

A sea of existences suffocated under the white of the page
Mirages of reflected images distant echoes of voices
The white of the page is not enough to disguise nothingness

The word expands stretches to wrap itself around the world
The white of the page is a sky traversed by a shudder
Like a watermark bearing the image of Washington

The emptiness swarms with similar larvae of words and unknowns
Mirages of the things of life lived under the dollar sign
A page that expands stretches to wrap itself around the world.

And Suddenly It's a Fiesta

There are many people who write poems, or more or less have written
　　them.
Maybe as a boy, "Counselor" Giovanni Agnelli, of Fiat
Fame, maybe President Nixon, certainly John Kennedy.
So let's subdivide "poets" in three distinct categories.

There's the Ineffable who writes words like nightingale, torment,
The Imponderable who says "the mutation of the clinamen",
The Irresponsible who experiments with new syntactic tangles

To these categories we add other *novissime*:
Who dabble with glue loudspeakers trumpets
Swollen tubes matches streamers phonographs.

All of them in various ways refurnish more perfect
Alibis for the old and new bosses, showing peole
That in this world still one things one enjoys one dreams

One lives to talk nonsense one suffers one torments oneself
Stabbed by a sciatica by a debt by a ray of sunlight,
One wets the finger to count change,
Without knowing either bulls or figs, and suddenly it's a fiesta.

(tr. Paul Vangelisti)

Patrizia Vicinelli

[*Fragmentation, ii*]

Carlo Villa

George Washington

Sometimes the captain feels unwell,
ill-tempered, or he likes to play the lunatic
as evidence of his immanent superiority;

only such a theory could explain
why he strode up and down the poop
avoiding the eyes of his lieutenant

who waited in the grip of dreadful anguish
for his leader's first glance;
until the latter finally declared:

"We've had no news this year
from Benjamin Franklin in Paris,
we must write him a letter."

In League with Things

We think with the mouth and tongue,
but not with earholes plugged.

We think for as long as we listen to words inside our head,
sotto voce, in league with things,

and the wind is a quick word
because it travels fast,

and the word elephant is so strong
it carries everything at once,

while the word to finish
is a spiderweb of frivolous things

that tear themselves apart, spi-der-web,
to reach a guarded happiness.

(tr. Margaret Straus)

Emilio Villa

HISSE TOI RE
D'AMOUR DA MOU RIRE

Romansexe
par Emilio Villa

Sixieme Edition
MCMXXI

I soirée

    les lèvres
    aveugles
    devenues

lèchent

le (les) (1) pierres–ensembles   ont di que tu es tu
lèche les lèvres du christianisme
    une Crampe Charnelle in corpore luteo

II soirée

SEE SAW
FACE TONE
PEDERSTALS
THROAT
BATTOM
SLEE EEP!

qu'   elle   ignore(ra)

ce

qu'est devenu son

Géniteur

aux diles tordues

ju   vén   îles

l'Incarnation qui mente se meurt
(se mord, mordre) (se merde) dans
son dedans, du son (je se mords)
(suis donc) (je suis mords)
(corpor and)
              (la toute étée, elle)

BED CHICKENS
BED CHICKENS
BED CHICKENS

un troubli troutotal
pénétrant, en salive refusée

III soirée

ne suis-je donc que   ?

(ou en   )

mais elle ne se verra foutre
soi–même   , soi l'autre,
dans la Vulve Plénaire,
Vulve Pleurante Etern   elle,

mi   roir

que quoi?   où   a?   hein?

quoi rien?

(et le Déordorant
Vulvemachie
sur la Sommité
Perpetuum)

IV soirée

TO BE SEEN

(ma proie
(ta troie, 3)
(ma toi,
    onde !)

Luigi Viola

Cesare Vivaldi

Striptease

> La bionda ballerina
> da pochi mesi femina
> danza ad orchestra piena . . . !
> Pompeo Bettini

1

Lily Niagara takes off the clothes perfumed with sleep. She gathers a net of pleats and feigned caresses.

Faces in the purple shadow like paper in the field where children nap.

A drum roll. She takes a step forward. A drum roll. She steps back. Rhythm of an elastic garter stretched and let go.

White flesh between black hair: the naked silk of a body in a cone of light. And the triumphal bump! The breasts almost thrown into the air. Their evasion of the flashing laws of gravity.

2

Child faces in the field where a shadow of purple paper naps.

Elastic rhythm of a garter of a step. A roll stretched forward and back: drum letting go.

Almost thrown into the triumphal gravity of the air read the laws flashing the white bump of the breasts. Naked light of the cone of a body of flesh evaded by the silk of the black hair.

Lily takes off a feigned Niagara of pleats. The clothes perfumed with caresses gathered in a net of sleep.

3

Drum of a roll of a stretched step that the elastic advances and steps back letting go.

Flashing light in the black evasion of air: cone thrown by a triumphant breast. Read the laws of a white gravity of flesh almost silk in the bump of the naked hair.

A sleep of pleats gathers a Niagara of perfumed caresses. Lily who takes off feigned nets of clothes.

Where paper naps in the field of purple shadow she turns still a child.

4

The white laws of gravity. Evasion of the breasts of light from the black bump of the air! Flesh and hair of silk almost thrown toward the triumph of a body unsheathed in a flashing cone.

Perfumed nets gathered caresses of pleats: a lilac Niagara of clothes taken off from sleep.

On the purple field of faces paper children nap the shadows.

To the drum rhythm of a garter: a roll stretched and let go that advances and steps back.

5

Takes off the nets from feigned perfumed pleats of clothes gathers caresses of sleep Lily Niagara.

Girl purple with shadow the paper of the field naps in faces.

A step advances and steps back of a drum roll. Rhythm of elastic stretched and let go of a garter.

Read the laws of a black gravity of flesh thrown into a white flashing cone of light. Naked bump of breasts almost evaded by the body in the air of silk of the triumphant hair.

(tr. Paul Vangelisti)

Cesare Viviani

on the outside

o

convention of arrogance of the score, it heats you
with the moss of the surprise and the restraint of the
capers filing away the pigtail litotes:
miura left unexpressed the cleft of the limb in
pali time homes the mussels to the Ignis Deborah
and you prepare the slope with the unraveled lines
recruited, three together too
almost the mud from which
you stretched the distances. If it had been a two-way approach
in addition, if it had included too the envious relative
I did avoid the mixture but if the asthenic ox retreats
just fancy Frater that, it barked, it crumbles
string and digestion
getting up twice on the terrace

oo

the rising on trust of the slope a day framework
crackled negroid to me you throng white coffee the lighting
doesn't go out, thank goodness the weighing doesn't exclude the cat snap
and dependent on the feri the godmother displays circling the cèrvice
I imagine it is to coming out the red mouth from the black snake
the tip-offs with the brake handed out
forty-one-year-old
the matter of the body fireman spectacularing himself the traffic just think
more ability and drizzly stand, negotia europea:
who will you pass the street-corner to because you want the salt to soak itsel
in cotton and fat or don't bother if a fine-looking flock
takes the monkey wrench

ooo

the arrow squirted itself by trade
the tale in progress heralds itself as the infinite in Mixed
Steam and the cast-iron block risks freezing Nadia
who yoked runs between sandcastles
that embarrass with the home maize field, good because she was a virgin
weighing as much as a farthing

o o o
o

you contain, Saffa gorged herself with overseas
you dissimulated the ether the tube of the fourteen rays
cannot be thinned out by the sea bream
it must be able to mingle with the hoopoe and the shattering
of the trick of the hexagons bathed above the annotations
it is a master key, a low dive goes the rounds for the dead suture
and numerous sambas intercepted by mimesis
make the stop at Bologna
suited to repeated carbide red

o o o
o o

if the hopeless prophet makes a shirt he gets up and cloaks himself in sloth
he fools himself he's near to the mark of the water with a subtle selector
but sitting and ironing the sly ball beyond that one
and with the lowly the slushy,
he didn't know how to prune to the right means he has turned grey bordeau
where the Risen One was at home in the builder's yard to say it was
        more Pontius
than what was soon to begin sulking in the wood. Tell him make him aware
how this felling made a mistake
about the ghosts every saturday and
you stand out stealthily

o o o
o o o

the basket for the authentication smiles back-watering at the notary's
drunkenness to sell his brilliantined new-born children honest
because of the bad egg caused by the cockscomb, the terse brigand
        abandoned
for an ice of rice on the white coat the practical filter
of the invitation is turned on its head
in bygone times one would have listened to the ladle
and sprinkling oneself around
receding boots much was certainty

o o o
o o o
o

extreme pillar what arrogance to surprise
the interception of pain of the semen's iron-bedstead
the letter sub escaped the half-closed rough stone work
as if it were tarantelled on the index
and to be   it captured you without sales point
only with the cockpit's toothpaste

o o o
o o o
o o

not crammed remind me where it is wet
and strikeladlingtoo it tucked itself in
yes indeed proclaimed the fairy of the twins
we are the transformed skin
down with basic educashion
and in the fallen boiled beef was the dot of the shirt-waister

o o o
o o o
o o o

mattress of crimes are not so close-packed
but how the single shade of the First Sentiment
interests itself in the slobbered old man
this, situashion, with the enamel of essence
there is the movement that of the mosquito

o o o
o o o
o o o
o

when the bora I had in push-cart
tore to pieces the greenery
mama told me mind the big menthol, soon after
I tried the brew
but I never thought I'd reach the saint

(*tr. Robert Miller*)

William Xerra

profilarsi i segni di una insufficienza cardiocircolatoria, che hanno reso ne-

Al primo controllo (giugno 1961), l'esame elettrocardiografi-
co dimostra un flutter... pratico, in... co... tecnico... arrventricolare
variabile (Fig. 2, A)... deve essere...
... mente e spontaneamente il... necessario... iniziare
una idonea terapia...
tenuto per tutta la...
ritmico... blocco...
... salva... rallentamento (150 ingran... menti) l'oro...
tivi. Le pause diasto...
za apprezzabil...
e avevano costantemente... durate uguale e di ...sco inferiore
a... di due intervalli P-P... punto di ...
... mosinusale (Fig. 2, B)...
... controllo a... del marzo 1962, le... illustrano invece
l'aritmia seno-atriale, che... presenta caratteri del tutto par-
ticolari e nuovi, in quanto alla pausa sinusale conseguono ora co-
stantemente una o più battute di evasione nodale (Fig. 2, C). Dal
punto di vista soggettivo...
brio emodinamico...
vertigine o di...
Dopo quasi due... (...
paziente viene...
tranti di tachicardia...
depone di venire...
... L'ultima crisi...
... periferici; ha...

... tachicardia...
... con flutter atriale ritmico, con rapporto a-V costante 2/1
(Fig. 2, D). Il parossismo tachisistolico da flutter atriale cessa

[ED : *In Italian, 'vive' = 'stet'*]

A publisher's note

This anthology is second in a series of current poetry; news of the first volume, *Humps & Wings: a selection of Polish Poetry Since '68,* will be found on page 128. The zero volume, *the first 25,* is forthcoming: a condensation of the tabloid *Invisible City* that Paul Vangelisti and I have edited since 1971 – 'a collection of poetry, translations, statements and visuals published whenever enough good material is available.' An eclectic line, to be continued (tabloid or book) as needed.

This anthology has been long in the press: Adriano Spatola and Giulia Niccolai first invited contributions in late 1977; the text was ready only in early 1981; a year of preparation and printing has taken its toll. We thank the poets and translators for their patience.

One previous anthology deserves special acknowledgment: Vittoria Bradshaw's *From Pure Silence to Impure Dialogue, a survey of Italian poetry 1945–1965.* Published by Las Americas (New York City, 1971), the anthology was never properly distributed – the few copies in circulation were rescued by the editor/translator from the bindery. The collection traces its theme from the twilight of hermeticism through the various 'realisms' of those twenty years down to the new avant-garde of 'i novissimi' and the 'verri' group. The Italian text of the poems is presented facing the translations, as well as a generous sampling of spirited criticism on and by the poets. A labor of love; Bradshaw may have a few copies left (4914 Park Ave, Riverside CA 92507).

Unlike the Polish volume (six poets illustrated by a single artist), this anthology includes some 76 poets, both visual and linear. It expands the selection of Italian poets found in the various past issues of the tabloid *Invisible City* – situating our frequent publication of the *tam-tam* poets (Spatola, Niccolai, Costa) whle narrowing the selection to the specifically (and perhaps self-consciously) experimental. Indeed in the first *Invisible City* (February 1971), Vangelisti published the first US translation of Spatola's "The Boomerang"; copies of that issue reached him and soon an exchange of books and texts resulted, culminating in this anthology – but continuing in #28 with a selection of poets & artists from *Cervo Volante,* the new broadside journal (published by Tomaso Cascella in Rome, and available in the USA from *Invisible City*) and with the forthcoming verse, *The Complete Films of Corrado Costa.*

This anthology documents the experiments of the 60s and 70s; a special collection in two respects: that the poets suggested their own selections and that visual work was fully incorporated into the anthology, not as illustration or decoration but as a precise research of certain of these poets. The twenty years covered are a complex panorama – Spatola & Vangelisti have provided an immediate background for the anthology, but a bibliography and author's notes would have been helpful. Unfortunately intercontinental publication on our budget rendered these amenities impossible. Readers might consult the interviews Niccolai and Spatola gave in *Invisible City* 23–25, explaining in particular their retreat to the country in the early 70s where they sustained a whole current of experiments in *tam-tam* and edizioni geiger.

One final point: the introduction to *The New Italian Poetry* (edited & translated by Lawrence Smith, University of California Press, 1981) concludes by quoting Philippe Sollers (he of *Tel Quel*); noting "both the enormous influence of the Italian avant-garde in the sixties and the suddenness of their decline in the seventies," Professor Smith quotes Sollers "...Yes, I'm talking about the avant-garde. I was amazed that during the period of our contacts with the 'Gruppo 63,' the Italians were perhaps even farther advanced than we were. Today I don't hear them anymore...." This lament for the 60s from the vantage of the mid-70s can be best countered by this volume of *Invisible City*. In its disparate, precise positions, *From Neo to Post Avant-garde* documents the Italian experiments of these years.

— *John McBride*

PS: One hates to quibble, but reading Professor Smith's notes, one would think that Spatola had published nothing since 1971, let alone had three translations published in the USA (in 1975, 1977 & 1978). Furthermore, Spatola hasn't lived in Bologna since 1964; after his years in Rome he and Giulia Niccolai retired to the country in the early 70's to publish *tam-tam* and edizioni geiger; he can still be addressed at: Mulino di Bazzano (Parma) 43020.

Other translations from the Italian by Paul Vangelisti published by Red Hill Press:

Franco Beltrametti: *Another Earthquake* (1976)
Corrado Costa: *Our Positions* (1975)
Giulia Niccolai: *Substitution* (1975)
Antonio Porta: *as if it were a rhythm* (1978)
Rocco Scotellaro: *The sky with its mouth wide open* (1976)
Vittorio Sereni: *Sixteen Poems* (1971)
Adriano Spatola: *Majakovskiiiiiiij* (1975)
                Zeroglyphics (prefatory matter to these visuals
                translated by PV and Giulia Niccolai, 1977)
                Various Devices (1978)

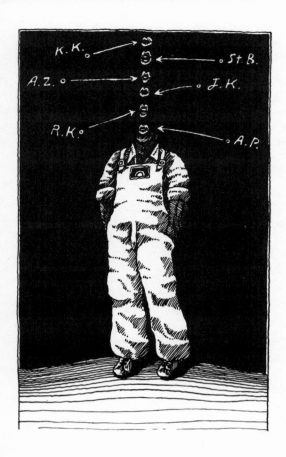

Invisible City | 1

Humps & Wings: Polish poetry since '68
edited by Tadeusz Nyczek, translated by Bogusław Rost-
worowski & illustrated by Jan Sawka – includes Krzysztof
Karasek, Stanisław Barańczak, Adam Zagajewski, Julian
Kornhauser, Ryszard Krynicki & Antoni Pawlak. (80 pages,
$5 postpaid if payment accompanies order)
    If this anthology of Italian experiments has (has not)
interested you, perhaps you'd like a very different volume
in the same series. Or perhaps one of the 50 titles on
the Red Hill Press backlist (Artaud, Vallejo, Perkoff,
Scotellaro, Thomas *et al*): send SSAE for a free sampler.
Or perhaps the continuing tabloid *Invisible City* ($3
postpaid.) Address:
   Invisible City / Red Hill Press
   PO Box 2853
   San Francisco, California 94126